Variations on a Theme

Granola

Lori Butler Carter

To Michael-san :
たのしんで ください !!!

ロ-リ-

Lori 12-1-09

This edition published by:

Sigma Software, Inc.
P.O Box 2311
Roswell, GA 30077
www.sigmasoftware.com

ISBN: 0-9763545-1-9

Table of Contents

Acknowledgements

When I first started making granola for my friends, they kept asking for the recipe. After a while I decided to write all of my recipes down so it would be easier to give them to my friends. As I was writing them I realized I had enough recipes for a small cookbook. So my first thank you is to all of my friends who asked for my granola recipes.

Since every recipe in this cookbook has been tested, many "guinea pigs" must be thanked.

To Rebecca and Joe – thank you for relieving my refrigerator of bag after bag of test granola.

To Mickey – thank you for being the ultimate guinea pig and testing "Honey Mustard".

And to Jeffery – many, many thanks for your terribly abused stomach, helpful opinions, and endless patience.

Introduction

Recipes are a lot like music. Just as each instrument in an orchestra plays the notes in a melody, each ingredient in a recipe adds its own notes to the food.

Sometimes there is a basic melody that leaps playfully from instrument to instrument. Though each section of the orchestra plays the same melody, the different instruments bring different textures to the sound and listeners are offered many versions of the same melody as it swirls around them in a variety of styles. These musical pieces are often called "variations on a theme".

This cookbook endeavors to offer its readers and tasters a symphony of flavors. Starting with the basic theme of a simple granola recipe, many variations are offered to please a plethora of palates.

Granola is a crunchy, tasty treat that can be enjoyed in many ways. Crumble it into milk for breakfast. Sprinkle the crumbles over pie or ice-cream for dessert. Break it into pieces and eat it with your lunch. Keep it around for a mid-day snack. Pack some in your backpack for an energy boost when you are hiking. Take some on long car trips or airplane flights so you can have a crunchy nibble available when you need it.

The best thing about making your own granola is the ultimate control you have. You can use the ingredients you like and the ingredients you want. And it is so easy to make and store, you can have several flavors on hand for everyone's tastes and needs!

About this book

In this cookbook you will learn a basic granola recipe followed by several variations of the basic recipe – variations on a theme of granola.

The recipes are grouped into four categories: Relatively Healthy, A Little Decadent, Really Weird, and Celebrations.

The recipes are presented in each category in alphabetical order based on the most prominent flavors in the recipe. To help you locate a recipe of interest, the index at the end of the book lists recipe names and individual ingredients.

The first recipe in this cookbook explains the basic ingredients and the instructions for making granola as well as some notes about ingredients.

Each of the other recipes list specific ingredients to create a variation of the basic recipe. The instructions for each recipe are the same as the first recipe, so only quick instructions are provided with every recipe. Just follow the basic instructions unless indicated otherwise.

You will find that there are only a few ingredients that do not change from recipe to recipe – rolled oats, wheat germ and brown sugar. The oats and the wheat germ are the base of the granola and the brown sugar helps hold it all together. Most of the other ingredients vary for the sake of flavor and texture, but they usually add up to about the same proportions.

You can use the ingredients and measurements in these recipes as they are written or you can change them a little bit here and there.

Once you have made a few batches of granola following the recipes in this book, you will be able to invent your own combinations. The variations are virtually endless.

So read the basic recipe first, select a variation, and enjoy!

Basic Recipe

Dry Ingredients:

Full Batch	Half Batch	
1 Cup	½ Cup	Old Fashioned Oats
1 Cup	½ Cup	Nuts (any kind, chopped or whole)
½ Cup	¼ Cup	Seeds (e.g. sunflower seeds)
½ Cup	¼ Cup	Wheat Germ

Cereal and Fruit:

Full Batch	Half Batch	
1 Cup	½ Cup	Crisp Rice Cereal (variations may use other cereals)
1 Cup	½ Cup	Dried Fruit (chopped or whole, e.g. raisins)

Wet Ingredients:

Full Batch	Half Batch	
1 Tablespoon	1 ½ Teaspoons	Butter (or margarine)
¼ Cup	2 Tablespoons	Brown Sugar (Light or Dark)
¼ Cup	2 Tablespoons	Honey
¼ Cup	2 Tablespoons	Maple Syrup
2 Teaspoons	1 Teaspoon	Vanilla Extract

Candy:
(Some variations use chocolate chips or other candies)

(1) Pre-heat oven to 300 degrees Fahrenheit.

(2) If the nuts, seeds, and/or wheat germ you are using are already roasted, you do not need to roast them again, otherwise, spread the nuts, seeds, and wheat germ on a 13" x 9" sheet pan for a full batch or an 8" x 8" pan for a half batch. Bake for 10 minutes. The roasting brings out the flavor of the nuts and seeds. You can roast the oats too; it adds a mild toasted flavor to them.

There are different kinds of rolled oats available. "Old Fashioned" oats take longer to cook versus "Quick Oats". Though quick oats can be used in this recipe, the old fashioned oats work better.

Nuts can be chopped or whole and the dried fruit can be chopped or whole, depending on the texture you prefer. If a recipe works particularly better with a chopped ingredient, the ingredient list will indicate specifically that the ingredient should be chopped.

(3) While the dry ingredients are roasting, measure the cereal and fruit into a large bowl.

(4) When the dry ingredients are roasted, add them to the cereal and fruit. Mix to combine.

(5) In a small saucepan, mix together the wet ingredients. Heat over medium heat stirring constantly until all of the sugar is melted and the mixture begins to bubble (about 5 minutes)

(6) Reduce the heat to low and continue heating until the mixture begins to thicken (about another 5 minutes)

The delicate flavor of some vanillas and other extracts can be affected by heat, so you may want to add them to the wet ingredients after the wet ingredients have been heated.

*Where honey, syrups, jams, jellies, and marmalades are concerned, it is better if you use natural or fruit juice sweetened products, but if you cannot find them, use regular versions. **Do not** use low sugar products or artificially sweetened products.*

(7) Cool the wet mixture slightly before pouring it over the dry mixture in the large bowl and mix to combine. A rubber or silicone spatula works best. **Caution: Syrup is very hot!**

(8) Since chocolate chips will melt when the wet ingredients are added, if a recipe uses candy it must be mixed in **after** the wet ingredients are fully incorporated.

(9) Prepare the sheet pan you used to roast the nuts by wiping vegetable oil on it or spray it with non-stick spray.

(10) Pour the granola mixture into the sheet pan and spread it evenly with a rubber or silicone spatula, but do not press it down unless directed to do so. This keeps the granola lighter and crisper.

(11) Bake at 300 degrees Fahrenheit for 25 minutes.

(12) Allow the granola to cool for at least 15 minutes or until it is still warm, but comfortable to touch.

(13) Place a cutting board on top of the sheet pan and invert the pan so the granola will come out. You may have to tap the pan to get the granola to release.

(14) Let the granola cool completely.

(15) Break the granola into about 1 inch by 1 inch pieces, or crumble into small pieces.

You can store this granola in plastic bags, plastic containers, or glass containers, but whatever type of container you choose, be sure it seals tightly.

This granola can be stored in the freezer for 4 to 6 months, in the refrigerator for 2 to 3 months, and at room temperature for 3 or 4 weeks.

Makes Approximately:

Full Batch – 40 Servings

Half Batch – 20 Servings

Chapter 1 – Relatively Healthy

All of the granolas in this cookbook have whole grains, even the decadent ones, but the difference between the recipes in this chapter and the recipes in Chapter 2 (A Little Decadent) is that the recipes in this chapter endeavor to keep the granola a little healthier.

These recipes encourage you to use crispy brown rice cereal and fruit juice sweetened jams and marmalades. Plus, they do not include ingredients like chocolate chips, marshmallows, cookies, or candy.

Even with an eye towards a healthier snack, the variations of granola in this chapter bring you bright, bold flavors that make them truly special!

Apple

Dry Ingredients (Bake at 300°F for 10 minutes):

Full Batch	Half Batch	
1 Cup	½ Cup	Old Fashioned Oats
1 Cup	½ Cup	Walnuts
½ Cup	¼ Cup	Sunflower Seeds
½ Cup	¼ Cup	Wheat Germ

Cereal and Fruit (Mix with dry ingredients):

Full Batch	Half Batch	
1 Cup	½ Cup	Crisp Brown Rice Cereal
1 Cup	½ Cup	Dried Apple (chopped)
½ Cup	¼ Cup	Raisins
1 Teaspoon	½ Teaspoon	Ground Cinnamon

Wet Ingredients (Melt in saucepan until thick):

Full Batch	Half Batch	
1 Tablespoon	1 ½ Teaspoons	Butter
¼ Cup	2 Tablespoons	Brown Sugar
¼ Cup	2 Tablespoons	Honey
¼ Cup	2 Tablespoons	Maple Syrup
1 Teaspoon	½ Teaspoon	Vanilla Extract

Caution: Syrup is very hot!

Mix wet ingredients with other ingredients, spread evenly in pan; bake at 300°F for 25 minutes.

This recipe combines dried apples and raisins instead of using only dried apples. For a stronger apple flavor substitute more dried apples for the raisins.

Apricot

Dry Ingredients (Bake at 300°F for 10 minutes):

Full Batch	Half Batch	
1 Cup	½ Cup	Old Fashioned Oats
1 Cup	½ Cup	Cashews
½ Cup	¼ Cup	Sunflower Seeds
½ Cup	¼ Cup	Wheat Germ

Cereal and Fruit (Mix with dry ingredients):

Full Batch	Half Batch	
1 Cup	½ Cup	Crisp Rice Cereal
1 Cup	½ Cup	Dried Apricots (chopped)

Wet Ingredients (Melt in saucepan until thick):

Full Batch	Half Batch	
1 Tablespoon	1 ½ Teaspoons	Butter
¼ Cup	2 Tablespoons	Brown Sugar
½ Cup	¼ Cup	Apricot Preserves
1 Teaspoon	½ Teaspoon	Vanilla Extract
1 Teaspoon	½ Teaspoon	Brandy Extract

Caution: Syrup is very hot!

Mix wet ingredients with other ingredients, spread evenly in pan and press firmly if the mixture is not sticky; bake at 300°F for 25 minutes.

Apricot jam or apricot preserves can be used for this granola. Fruit juice sweetened products are best, but sugar or corn syrup sweetened products are fine too. Just don't use low sugar or no sugar products.

Banana Bread

Dry Ingredients (Bake at 300°F for 10 minutes):

Full Batch	Half Batch	
1 Cup	½ Cup	Old Fashioned Oats
½ Cup	¼ Cup	Pecans
1 Cup	½ Cup	Walnuts
½ Cup	¼ Cup	Wheat Germ

Cereal and Fruit (Mix with dry ingredients):

Full Batch	Half Batch	
1 Cup	½ Cup	Crisp Brown Rice Cereal
½ Cup	¼ Cup	Raisins
1 Cup	½ Cup	Dried Banana Chips (chopped)
1 Teaspoon	½ Teaspoon	Ground Cinnamon

Wet Ingredients (Melt in saucepan until thick):

Full Batch	Half Batch	
1 Tablespoon	1 ½ Teaspoons	Butter
¼ Cup	2 Tablespoons	Brown Sugar
¼ Cup	2 Tablespoons	Honey
¼ Cup	2 Tablespoons	Maple Syrup
1 Tablespoon	1 ½ Teaspoons	Banana Extract
1 Teaspoon	½ Teaspoon	Vanilla Extract

<u>Caution</u>: **Syrup is very hot!**

Mix wet ingredients with other ingredients, spread evenly in pan; bake at 300°F for 25 minutes.

Break the banana chips into small pieces so they can disperse throughout the granola better.

Blueberry

Dry Ingredients (Bake at 300°F for 10 minutes):

Full Batch	Half Batch	
1 Cup	½ Cup	Old Fashioned Oats
1 Cup	½ Cup	Pecans
½ Cup	¼ Cup	Pumpkin Seeds
½ Cup	¼ Cup	Wheat Germ

Cereal and Fruit (Mix with dry ingredients):

Full Batch	Half Batch	
1 Cup	½ Cup	Crisp Brown Rice Cereal
1 Cup	½ Cup	Dried Blueberries
1 Teaspoon	½ Teaspoon	Lemon Zest
¼ Teaspoon	1/8 Teaspoon	Ground Cinnamon

Wet Ingredients (Melt in saucepan until thick):

Full Batch	Half Batch	
1 Tablespoon	1 ½ Teaspoons	Butter
¼ Cup	2 Tablespoons	Brown Sugar
¼ Cup	2 Tablespoons	Honey
¼ Cup	2 Tablespoons	Maple Syrup
1 Teaspoon	½ Teaspoon	Vanilla Extract

<u>Caution</u>: Syrup is very hot!

Mix wet ingredients with other ingredients, spread evenly in pan; bake at 300°F for 25 minutes.

A hint of cinnamon and lemon in this granola help bring out the flavor of the blueberries and makes it reminiscent of blueberry pie.

To zest the lemon use a grater like you would use for cheese and use the finest grate you can. Make sure to remove only the colored part of the skin because the white part (called the pith) is bitter.

Carrot Pineapple Raisin

Dry Ingredients (Bake at 300°F for 10 minutes):

Full Batch	Half Batch	
1 Cup	½ Cup	Old Fashioned Oats
1 Cup	½ Cup	Pecans
½ Cup	¼ Cup	Pumpkin Seeds
½ Cup	¼ Cup	Wheat Germ

Cereal and Fruit (Mix with dry ingredients):

Full Batch	Half Batch	
1 Cup	½ Cup	Crisp Brown Rice Cereal
½ Cup	¼ Cup	Raisins
1 Cup	½ Cup	Dried Pineapple (chopped)

Wet Ingredients (Melt in saucepan until thick):

Full Batch	Half Batch	
1 Tablespoon	1 ½ Teaspoons	Butter
¼ Cup	2 Tablespoons	Brown Sugar
¼ Cup	2 Tablespoons	Honey
¼ Cup	2 Tablespoons	Maple Syrup
1 Cup	½ Cup	Carrots (shredded/grated)
2 Teaspoons	1 Teaspoon	Vanilla Extract

Caution: Syrup is very hot!

Mix wet ingredients with other ingredients, spread evenly in pan and press firmly if the mixture is not sticky; bake at 300°F for 25 minutes.

Notice the carrots are cooked with the wet ingredients rather than mixed in with the dry ingredients to ensure they are not too wet. The syrup will take longer to thicken than in most of the other recipes, so be sure to allow plenty of time to cook it. Because the carrots are fresh, not dried, this granola must be refrigerated.

Cherry Almond

Dry Ingredients (Bake at 300°F for 10 minutes):

Full Batch	Half Batch	
1 Cup	½ Cup	Old Fashioned Oats
1 Cup	½ Cup	Slivered Almonds
½ Cup	¼ Cup	Pumpkin Seeds
½ Cup	¼ Cup	Wheat Germ

Cereal and Fruit (Mix with dry ingredients):

Full Batch	Half Batch	
1 Cup	½ Cup	Crisp Brown Rice Cereal
1 Cup	½ Cup	Dried Cherries (Chopped)

Wet Ingredients (Melt in saucepan until thick):

Full Batch	Half Batch	
1 Tablespoon	1 ½ Teaspoons	Butter
¼ Cup	2 Tablespoons	Brown Sugar
2 Tablespoons	1 Tablespoon	Honey
½ Cup	¼ Cup	Cherry Preserves
4 Teaspoons	2 Teaspoons	Almond Extract

<u>Caution</u>: **Syrup is very hot!**

Mix wet ingredients with other ingredients, spread evenly in pan and press firmly if the mixture is not sticky; bake at 300°F for 25 minutes.

The slivered almonds and the almond extract in this granola help enhance the flavor of the dried cherries. Fruit juice sweetened preserves work best in this recipe, but if you can't find any, regular preserves are fine; however, **do not** use preserves made with artificial sweeteners or low sugar preserves. Also, be sure to cook the wet ingredients until the sauce thickens slightly or the granola may be a little wet or soggy.

Chocolate Banana

Dry Ingredients (Bake at 300°F for 10 minutes):

Full Batch	Half Batch	
1 Cup	½ Cup	Old Fashioned Oats
1 Cup	½ Cup	Walnuts
½ Cup	¼ Cup	Pumpkin Seeds
½ Cup	¼ Cup	Wheat Germ

Cereal and Fruit (Mix with dry ingredients):

Full Batch	Half Batch	
1 Cup	½ Cup	Crisp Brown Rice Cereal
1 Cup	½ Cup	Dried Banana Chips (chopped)
½ Cup	¼ Cup	Golden Raisins

Wet Ingredients (Melt in saucepan until thick):

Full Batch	Half Batch	
1 Tablespoon	1 ½ Teaspoons	Butter
¼ Cup	2 Tablespoons	Brown Sugar
¼ Cup	2 Tablespoons	Honey
¼ Cup	2 Tablespoons	Maple Syrup
2 Teaspoons	1 Teaspoon	Unsweetened Cocoa
2 Teaspoons	1 Teaspoon	Banana Extract
1 Teaspoon	½ Teaspoon	Vanilla Extract

Caution: Syrup is very hot!

Mix wet ingredients with other ingredients, spread evenly in pan; bake at 300°F for 25 minutes.

Add chocolate chips – ½ cup (¼ cup for half batch) to make this granola little less healthy and a little more decadent, but cool the wet ingredients slightly before adding to the dry ingredients and add the chocolate chips last, stirring quickly.

Chocolate Mint

Dry Ingredients (Bake at 300°F for 10 minutes):

Full Batch	Half Batch	
1 Cup	½ Cup	Old Fashioned Oats
1 Cup	½ Cup	Pecans
½ Cup	¼ Cup	Pumpkin Seeds
½ Cup	¼ Cup	Wheat Germ

Cereal and Fruit (Mix with dry ingredients):

Full Batch	Half Batch	
1 Cup	½ Cup	Crisp Brown Rice Cereal
½ Cup	¼ Cup	Raisins
½ Cup	¼ Cup	Golden Raisins

Wet Ingredients (Melt in saucepan until thick):

Full Batch	Half Batch	
1 Tablespoon	1 ½ Teaspoons	Butter
¼ Cup	2 Tablespoons	Brown Sugar
¼ Cup	2 Tablespoons	Honey
¼ Cup	2 Tablespoons	Maple Syrup
2 Teaspoons	1 Teaspoon	Unsweetened Cocoa
1 Teaspoon	½ Teaspoon	Instant Coffee Granules
1 Teaspoon	½ Teaspoon	Vanilla Extract
1 Teaspoon	½ Teaspoon	Peppermint Extract

<u>Caution</u>: **Syrup is very hot!**

Mix wet ingredients with other ingredients, spread evenly in pan; bake at 300°F for 25 minutes.

Chocolatey, minty, crunchy, yummy!!!

An unexpected ingredient, a little bit of coffee intensifies the flavor of chocolate.

Cinnamon Raisin

Dry Ingredients (Bake at 300°F for 10 minutes):

Full Batch	Half Batch	
1 Cup	½ Cup	Old Fashioned Oats
1 Cup	½ Cup	Pecans
½ Cup	¼ Cup	Sunflower Seeds
½ Cup	¼ Cup	Wheat Germ

Cereal and Fruit (Mix with dry ingredients):

Full Batch	Half Batch	
1 Cup	½ Cup	Crisp Brown Rice Cereal
1 Cup	½ Cup	Raisins
2 Teaspoons	1 Teaspoon	Ground Cinnamon

Wet Ingredients (Melt in saucepan until thick):

Full Batch	Half Batch	
1 Tablespoon	1 ½ Teaspoons	Butter
¼ Cup	2 Tablespoons	Brown Sugar
¼ Cup	2 Tablespoons	Honey
¼ Cup	2 Tablespoons	Maple Syrup
1 Teaspoon	½ Teaspoon	Vanilla Extract

<u>Caution</u>: Syrup is very hot!

Mix wet ingredients with other ingredients, spread evenly in pan; bake at 300°F for 25 minutes.

The cinnamon in this granola complements the raisins wonderfully, but for a less intense cinnamon flavor, just reduce the cinnamon from 2 teaspoons to 1 teaspoon (½ teaspoon for a half batch).

Coconut Almond

Dry Ingredients (Bake at 300°F for 10 minutes):

Full Batch	Half Batch	
1 Cup	½ Cup	Old Fashioned Oats
1 Cup	½ Cup	Slivered Almonds
½ Cup	¼ Cup	Pumpkin Seeds
½ Cup	¼ Cup	Wheat Germ

Cereal and Fruit (Mix with dry ingredients):

Full Batch	Half Batch	
1 Cup	½ Cup	Crisp Brown Rice Cereal
½ Cup	¼ Cup	Golden Raisins
1 Cup	½ Cup	Shredded Coconut

Wet Ingredients (Melt in saucepan until thick):

Full Batch	Half Batch	
1 Tablespoon	1 ½ Teaspoons	Butter
¼ Cup	2 Tablespoons	Brown Sugar
¼ Cup	2 Tablespoons	Honey
¼ Cup	2 Tablespoons	Maple Syrup
2 Teaspoons	1 Teaspoon	Unsweetened Cocoa
1 Teaspoon	½ Teaspoon	Vanilla Extract
1 Teaspoon	½ Teaspoon	Almond Extract

<u>Caution</u>: Syrup is very hot!

Mix wet ingredients with other ingredients, spread evenly in pan; bake at 300°F for 25 minutes.

This chocolate, coconut, and almond combination is a "joy" to make and a "joy" to eat! Use dark chocolate cocoa to make this granola extra special!

Cranberry Orange

Dry Ingredients (Bake at 300°F for 10 minutes):

Full Batch	Half Batch	
1 Cup	½ Cup	Old Fashioned Oats
1 Cup	½ Cup	Pecans
½ Cup	¼ Cup	Pumpkin Seeds
½ Cup	¼ Cup	Wheat Germ

Cereal and Fruit (Mix with dry ingredients):

Full Batch	Half Batch	
1 Cup	½ Cup	Crisp Brown Rice Cereal
1 Cup	½ Cup	Dried Cranberries

Wet Ingredients (Melt in saucepan until thick):

Full Batch	Half Batch	
1 Tablespoon	1 ½ Teaspoons	Butter
¼ Cup	2 Tablespoons	Brown Sugar
½ Cup	¼ Cup	Orange Marmalade
2 Teaspoons	1 Teaspoon	Vanilla Extract

Caution: Syrup is very hot!

Mix wet ingredients with other ingredients, spread evenly in pan and press firmly if the mixture is not sticky; bake at 300°F for 25 minutes.

Fruit juice sweetened orange marmalade works best in this recipe, but if you can't find any, regular orange marmalade is fine; however, **do not** use marmalade made with artificial sweeteners or low sugar marmalade.

Date Nut

Dry Ingredients (Bake at 300°F for 10 minutes):

Full Batch	Half Batch	
1 Cup	½ Cup	Old Fashioned Oats
1 Cup	½ Cup	Pecans
½ Cup	¼ Cup	Pumpkin Seeds
½ Cup	¼ Cup	Wheat Germ

Cereal and Fruit (Mix with dry ingredients):

Full Batch	Half Batch	
1 Cup	½ Cup	Crisp Brown Rice Cereal
½ Cup	¼ Cup	Dried Dates (Chopped)
½ Cup	¼ Cup	Dried Cherries (Chopped)

Wet Ingredients (Melt in saucepan until thick):

Full Batch	Half Batch	
1 Tablespoon	1 ½ Teaspoons	Butter
¼ Cup	2 Tablespoons	Brown Sugar
¼ Cup	2 Tablespoons	Honey
¼ Cup	2 Tablespoons	Maple Syrup
1 Teaspoon	½ Teaspoon	Vanilla Extract
1 Teaspoon	½ Teaspoon	Almond Extract

<u>Caution</u>: **Syrup is very hot!**

Mix wet ingredients with other ingredients, spread evenly in pan; bake at 300°F for 25 minutes.

The cherries in this granola complement the dates as they add additional texture and chewiness, but if you want more date flavor, substitute dates for the cherries.

Ginger Sesame

Dry Ingredients (Bake at 300°F for 10 minutes):

Full Batch	Half Batch	
1 Cup	½ Cup	Old Fashioned Oats
1 Cup	½ Cup	Cashews
¼ Cup	2 Tablespoons	Pumpkin Seeds
¼ Cup	2 Tablespoons	Sesame Seeds
½ Cup	¼ Cup	Wheat Germ

Cereal and Fruit (Mix with dry ingredients):

Full Batch	Half Batch	
1 Cup	½ Cup	Crisp Brown Rice Cereal
½ Cup	¼ Cup	Crystallized Ginger (chopped)
½ Cup	¼ Cup	Golden Raisins

Wet Ingredients (Melt in saucepan until thick):

Full Batch	Half Batch	
1 Tablespoon	1 ½ Teaspoons	Butter
¼ Cup	2 Tablespoons	Brown Sugar
¼ Cup	2 Tablespoons	Honey
¼ Cup	2 Tablespoons	Maple Syrup
2 Teaspoons	1 Teaspoon	Vanilla Extract

Caution: Syrup is very hot!

Mix wet ingredients with other ingredients, spread evenly in pan; bake at 300°F for 25 minutes.

Since it has a very strong, intense flavor, be sure to chop the crystallized ginger in very small pieces so it is distributed throughout the granola.

If you prefer a stronger sesame flavor, double the sesame seeds and omit the pumpkin seeds

GORP (Good Old Raisins & Peanuts)

Dry Ingredients (Bake at 300°F for 10 minutes):

Full Batch	Half Batch	
1 Cup	½ Cup	Old Fashioned Oats
1 Cup	½ Cup	Peanuts (salted)
½ Cup	¼ Cup	Sunflower Seeds
½ Cup	¼ Cup	Wheat Germ

Cereal and Fruit (Mix with dry ingredients):

Full Batch	Half Batch	
1 Cup	½ Cup	Crisp Brown Rice Cereal
1 Cup	½ Cup	Raisins

Wet Ingredients (Melt in saucepan until thick):

Full Batch	Half Batch	
1 Tablespoon	1 ½ Teaspoons	Butter
¼ Cup	2 Tablespoons	Brown Sugar
¼ Cup	2 Tablespoons	Honey
¼ Cup	2 Tablespoons	Maple Syrup
2 Teaspoons	1 Teaspoon	Vanilla Extract

Caution: Syrup is very hot!

Mix wet ingredients with other ingredients, spread evenly in pan; bake at 300°F for 25 minutes.

GORP, good old raisins and peanuts, is popular with hikers because it is easy to carry and provides a healthy energy boost. This granola version is a tasty twist on the classic hiking snack.

You can use either salted or unsalted peanuts depending on your taste, but if you are not sure, try it with salted peanuts. They add an interesting contrast to the sweetness of the raisins.

Lemon Lime

Dry Ingredients (Bake at 300°F for 10 minutes):

Full Batch	Half Batch	
1 Cup	½ Cup	Old Fashioned Oats
1 Cup	½ Cup	Pecans
½ Cup	¼ Cup	Pumpkin Seeds
½ Cup	¼ Cup	Wheat Germ

Cereal and Fruit (Mix with dry ingredients):

Full Batch	Half Batch	
1 Cup	½ Cup	Crisp Rice Cereal
1 Cup	½ Cup	Golden Raisins
1 Tablespoon	1 ½ Teaspoons	Lemon Zest
1 Tablespoon	1 ½ Teaspoons	Lime Zest

Wet Ingredients (Melt in saucepan until thick):

Full Batch	Half Batch	
1 Tablespoon	1 ½ Teaspoons	Butter
¼ Cup	2 Tablespoons	Brown Sugar
¼ Cup	2 Tablespoons	Honey
¼ Cup	2 Tablespoons	Maple Syrup
1 Teaspoon	½ Teaspoon	Vanilla Extract

<u>Caution</u>: Syrup is very hot!

Mix wet ingredients with other ingredients, spread evenly in pan; bake at 300°F for 25 minutes.

The lemon zest and lime zest bring bright, fresh notes to this granola.

To zest the fruit use a grater like you would use for cheese and use the finest grate you can. Make sure to remove only the colored part of the skin because the white part (called the pith) is bitter.

Maple

Dry Ingredients (Bake at 300°F for 10 minutes):

Full Batch	Half Batch	
1 Cup	½ Cup	Old Fashioned Oats
½ Cup	¼ Cup	Cashews
½ Cup	¼ Cup	Walnuts
½ Cup	¼ Cup	Pumpkin Seeds
½ Cup	¼ Cup	Wheat Germ

Cereal and Fruit (Mix with dry ingredients):

Full Batch	Half Batch	
1 Cup	½ Cup	Crisp Brown Rice Cereal
1 Cup	½ Cup	Golden Raisins

Wet Ingredients (Melt in saucepan until thick):

Full Batch	Half Batch	
1 Tablespoon	1 ½ Teaspoons	Butter
¼ Cup	2 Tablespoons	Brown Sugar
½ Cup	¼ Cup	Maple Syrup
2 Teaspoons	1 Teaspoon	Maple Flavoring
1 Teaspoon	½ Teaspoon	Vanilla Extract

<u>Caution</u>: Syrup is very hot!

Mix wet ingredients with other ingredients, spread evenly in pan; bake at 300°F for 25 minutes.

Cashews and walnuts are a nice combination in general but with maple syrup and vanilla they make a great combination in this granola!

Nut & Honey

Dry Ingredients (Bake at 300°F for 10 minutes):

Full Batch	Half Batch	
1 Cup	½ Cup	Old Fashioned Oats
1 Cup	½ Cup	Honey Roasted Peanuts
½ Cup	¼ Cup	Sunflower Seeds
½ Cup	¼ Cup	Wheat Germ

Cereal and Fruit (Mix with dry ingredients):

Full Batch	Half Batch	
1 Cup	½ Cup	Crisp Brown Rice Cereal
1 Cup	½ Cup	Toasted Oat Cereal
1 Cup	½ Cup	Raisins

Wet Ingredients (Melt in saucepan until thick):

Full Batch	Half Batch	
1 Tablespoon	1 ½ Teaspoons	Butter
¼ Cup	2 Tablespoons	Brown Sugar
½ Cup	¼ Cup	Honey
2 Teaspoons	1 Teaspoon	Vanilla Extract

<u>Caution</u>: Syrup is very hot!

Mix wet ingredients with other ingredients, spread evenly in pan; bake at 300°F for 25 minutes.

The simple flavors in this recipe make it a great granola for taking on a hiking trip.

Peanut & Chocolate

Dry Ingredients (Bake at 300°F for 10 minutes):

Full Batch	Half Batch	
1 Cup	½ Cup	Old Fashioned Oats
1 Cup	½ Cup	Peanuts (unsalted)
½ Cup	¼ Cup	Sunflower Seeds
½ Cup	¼ Cup	Wheat Germ

Cereal and Fruit (Mix with dry ingredients):

Full Batch	Half Batch	
1 Cup	½ Cup	Chocolate Crisp Rice Cereal
1 Cup	½ Cup	Golden Raisins

Wet Ingredients (Melt in saucepan until thick):

Full Batch	Half Batch	
1 Tablespoon	1 ½ Teaspoons	Butter
¼ Cup	2 Tablespoons	Brown Sugar
¼ Cup	2 Tablespoons	Honey
¼ Cup	2 Tablespoons	Maple Syrup
2 Tablespoons	1 Tablespoon	Peanut Butter (at end)
2 Teaspoons	1 Teaspoon	Vanilla Extract

<u>Caution</u>: **Syrup is very hot!**

Mix wet ingredients with other ingredients, spread evenly in pan; bake at 300°F for 25 minutes.

Add the peanut butter at the end of the cooking process, just before you combine the wet ingredients to the dry ingredients.

If you want to make this granola a little naughty, cool the syrup slightly before adding it to the mix, then add ½ cup of chocolate chips (¼ cup for a half batch) stirring quickly so the chocolate doesn't melt.

Trail Mix

Dry Ingredients (Bake at 300°F for 10 minutes):

Full Batch	Half Batch	
1 Cup	½ Cup	Old Fashioned Oats
½ Cup	¼ Cup	Cashews
½ Cup	¼ Cup	Pecans
½ Cup	¼ Cup	Walnuts
¼ Cup	2 Tablespoons	Pumpkin Seeds
¼ Cup	2 Tablespoons	Sunflower Seeds
½ Cup	¼ Cup	Wheat Germ

Cereal and Fruit (Mix with dry ingredients):

Full Batch	Half Batch	
½ Cup	¼ Cup	Crisp Brown Rice Cereal
½ Cup	¼ Cup	Toasted Oat Cereal
¼ Cup	2 Tablespoons	Dried Papaya (chopped)
¼ Cup	2 Tablespoons	Dried Pineapple (chopped)
¼ Cup	2 Tablespoons	Dried Cranberries
¼ Cup	2 Tablespoons	Raisins

Wet Ingredients (Melt in saucepan until thick):

Full Batch	Half Batch	
1 Tablespoon	1 ½ Teaspoons	Butter
¼ Cup	2 Tablespoons	Brown Sugar
¼ Cup	2 Tablespoons	Honey
¼ Cup	2 Tablespoons	Maple Syrup
2 Teaspoons	1 Teaspoon	Vanilla Extract

<u>Caution</u>: **Syrup is very hot! Mix wet ingredients with other ingredients, spread evenly in pan; bake at 300°F for 25 minutes.**

Just as you can make your own trail mix using the combination of nuts, dried fruits, and cereals you like, you can choose your own combination of nuts, dried fruits, and cereal for trail mix granola!

Tropical

Dry Ingredients (Bake at 300°F for 10 minutes):

Full Batch	Half Batch	
1 Cup	½ Cup	Old Fashioned Oats
½ Cup	¼ Cup	Cashews
½ Cup	¼ Cup	Macadamia Nuts
½ Cup	¼ Cup	Pumpkin Seeds
½ Cup	¼ Cup	Wheat Germ

Cereal and Fruit (Mix with dry ingredients):

Full Batch	Half Batch	
1 Cup	½ Cup	Crisp Brown Rice Cereal
½ Cup	¼ Cup	Shredded Coconut
¼ Cup	2 Tablespoons	Dried Banana Chips (chopped)
¼ Cup	2 Tablespoons	Dried Mango (chopped)
¼ Cup	2 Tablespoons	Dried Papaya (chopped)
¼ Cup	2 Tablespoons	Dried Pineapple (chopped)

Wet Ingredients (Melt in saucepan until thick):

Full Batch	Half Batch	
1 Tablespoon	1 ½ Teaspoons	Butter
¼ Cup	2 Tablespoons	Brown Sugar
¼ Cup	2 Tablespoons	Honey
¼ Cup	2 Tablespoons	Maple Syrup
1 Teaspoon	½ Teaspoon	Banana Extract
1 Teaspoon	½ Teaspoon	Vanilla Extract

<u>Caution:</u> **Syrup is very hot! Mix wet ingredients with other ingredients, spread evenly in pan; bake at 300°F for 25 minutes.**

A variety of dried fruits really brightens the flavors of this granola and transports your taste buds to a sunny beach. All you need now is a little paper umbrella!

Chapter 2 – A Little Decadent

Granola is usually reasonably healthy, but it is possible to make it a little decadent.

The recipes in this chapter have ingredients like chocolate chips, cookies, marshmallows, and other candy. Though perhaps not quite as decadent as their names might suggest, these variations are certainly decadent for granola!

Banana Split

Dry Ingredients (Bake at 300°F for 10 minutes):

Full Batch	Half Batch	
1 Cup	½ Cup	Old Fashioned Oats
1 Cup	½ Cup	Pecans
½ Cup	¼ Cup	Pumpkin Seeds
½ Cup	¼ Cup	Wheat Germ

Cereal and Fruit (Mix with dry ingredients):

Full Batch	Half Batch	
1 Cup	½ Cup	Crisp Rice Cereal
¼ Cup	2 Tablespoons	Dried Banana Chips (chopped)
½ Cup	¼ Cup	Dried Pineapple (chopped)

Wet Ingredients (<u>Caution</u>: Syrup is very hot! Melt in saucepan until thick, cool slightly, add to mix):

Full Batch	Half Batch	
1 Tablespoon	1 ½ Teaspoons	Butter
¼ Cup	2 Tablespoons	Brown Sugar
2 Tablespoons	1 Tablespoon	Honey
2 Tablespoons	1 Tablespoon	Maple Syrup
½ Cup	¼ Cup	Strawberry Jam
2 Teaspoons	1 Teaspoon	Banana Extract
1 Teaspoon	½ Teaspoon	Vanilla Extract

Candy (Add to mix <u>after</u> wet ingredients have been mixed in):

Full Batch	Half Batch	
¼ Cup	2 Tablespoons	Semi-sweet Chocolate Chips
¼ Cup	2 Tablespoons	White Chocolate Chips

Spread evenly in pan and press firmly; bake at 300°F for 25 minutes. Cook wet ingredients until thick or the granola may be mushy or sticky.

Cherry Cordial

Dry Ingredients (Bake at 300°F for 10 minutes):

Full Batch	Half Batch	
1 Cup	½ Cup	Old Fashioned Oats
1 Cup	½ Cup	Slivered Almonds
½ Cup	¼ Cup	Pumpkin Seeds
½ Cup	¼ Cup	Wheat Germ

Cereal and Fruit (Mix with dry ingredients):

Full Batch	Half Batch	
1 Cup	½ Cup	Chocolate Crisp Rice Cereal
1 Cup	½ Cup	Candied Cherries (Chopped)

Wet Ingredients (<u>Caution</u>: Syrup is very hot! Melt in saucepan until thick, cool slightly, add to mix):

Full Batch	Half Batch	
1 Tablespoon	1 ½ Teaspoons	Butter
¼ Cup	2 Tablespoons	Brown Sugar
2 Tablespoons	1 Tablespoon	Honey
½ Cup	¼ Cup	Cherry Preserves
1 Teaspoon	½ Teaspoon	Vanilla Extract
2 Teaspoons	1 Teaspoon	Almond Extract

Candy (Add to mix <u>after</u> wet ingredients have been mixed in):

Full Batch	Half Batch	
¼ Cup	2 Tablespoons	Semi-sweet Chocolate Chips
½ Cup	2 Tablespoons	White Chocolate Chips

Spread evenly in pan and press firmly if the mixture is not sticky; bake at 300°F for 25 minutes.

Perhaps not as decadent as a real chocolate cherry cordial, but it is certainly a delightful treat! Don't use maraschino cherries – too wet.

Chocolate Candy

Dry Ingredients (Bake at 300°F for 10 minutes):

Full Batch	Half Batch	
1 Cup	½ Cup	Old Fashioned Oats
1 Cup	½ Cup	Cashews
½ Cup	¼ Cup	Pumpkin Seeds
½ Cup	¼ Cup	Wheat Germ

Cereal and Fruit (Mix with dry ingredients):

Full Batch	Half Batch	
1 Cup	½ Cup	Crisp Rice Cereal
½ Cup	¼ Cup	Golden Raisins

Wet Ingredients (<u>Caution</u>: Syrup is very hot! Melt in saucepan until thick, cool slightly, add to mix):

Full Batch	Half Batch	
1 Tablespoon	1 ½ Teaspoons	Butter
¼ Cup	2 Tablespoons	Brown Sugar
¼ Cup	2 Tablespoons	Honey
¼ Cup	2 Tablespoons	Maple Syrup
2 Teaspoons	1 Teaspoon	Vanilla Extract

Candy (Add to mix <u>after</u> wet ingredients have been mixed in):

Full Batch	Half Batch	
1 Cup –or–	½ Cup –or–	Candy Coated Chocolate –or–
½ Cup	¼ Cup	Mini Candy Coated Chocolate

Spread evenly in pan; bake at 300°F for 25 minutes.

Mm, candy coated chocolate, "mm"! Try it with flavors like peanut, almond, dark chocolate, etc. This granola is not as suitable for hiking or other warm environments because even though the chocolate won't melt in your hands, it might melt in your backpack, pocket…

Chocolate Chip

Dry Ingredients (Bake at 300°F for 10 minutes):

Full Batch	Half Batch	
1 Cup	½ Cup	Old Fashioned Oats
1 Cup	½ Cup	Pecans
½ Cup	¼ Cup	Pumpkin Seeds
½ Cup	¼ Cup	Wheat Germ

Cereal and Fruit (Mix with dry ingredients):

Full Batch	Half Batch	
1 Cup	½ Cup	Crisp Rice Cereal
1 Cup	½ Cup	Chocolate Chip Cookies (chopped)
½ Cup	¼ Cup	Raisins

Wet Ingredients (<u>Caution</u>: Syrup is very hot! Melt in saucepan until thick, cool slightly, add to mix):

Full Batch	Half Batch	
1 Tablespoon	1 ½ Teaspoons	Butter
¼ Cup	2 Tablespoons	Brown Sugar
¼ Cup	2 Tablespoons	Honey
¼ Cup	2 Tablespoons	Maple Syrup
2 Teaspoons	1 Teaspoon	Vanilla Extract

Candy (Add to mix <u>after</u> wet ingredients have been mixed in):

Full Batch	Half Batch	
½ Cup	¼ Cup	Semi-sweet Chocolate Chips

Spread evenly in pan; bake at 300°F for 25 minutes.

The very thing that makes this granola so special, the chocolate chips, make it not as suitable for hiking or other warm environments because the chocolate can melt and make a big mess!

Chocolate Chocolate

Dry Ingredients (Bake at 300°F for 10 minutes):

Full Batch	Half Batch	
1 Cup	½ Cup	Old Fashioned Oats
1 Cup	½ Cup	Pecans
½ Cup	¼ Cup	Pumpkin Seeds
½ Cup	¼ Cup	Wheat Germ

Cereal and Fruit (Mix with dry ingredients):

Full Batch	Half Batch	
1 ½ Cups	3/4 Cup	Chocolate Crisp Rice Cereal

Wet Ingredients (<u>Caution</u>: Syrup is very hot! Melt in saucepan until thick, cool slightly, add to mix):

Full Batch	Half Batch	
1 Tablespoon	1 ½ Teaspoons	Butter
¼ Cup	2 Tablespoons	Brown Sugar
¼ Cup	2 Tablespoons	Honey
¼ Cup	2 Tablespoons	Maple Syrup
1 Teaspoon	½ Teaspoon	Instant Coffee Granules
2 Teaspoons	1 Teaspoon	Unsweetened Cocoa
2 Teaspoons	1 Teaspoon	Vanilla Extract

Candy (Add to mix <u>after</u> wet ingredients have been mixed in):

Full Batch	Half Batch	
½ Cup	¼ Cup	Chocolate Covered Raisins
¼ Cup	2 Tablespoons	Candy Coated Chocolate
¼ Cup	2 Tablespoons	Semi-sweet Chocolate Chips
¼ Cup	2 Tablespoons	White Chocolate Chips

Spread evenly in pan; bake at 300°F for 25 minutes.

As much chocolate as you can cram into one granola!

Cookies & Cream

Dry Ingredients (Bake at 300°F for 10 minutes):

Full Batch	Half Batch	
1 Cup	½ Cup	Old Fashioned Oats
1 Cup	½ Cup	Pecans
½ Cup	¼ Cup	Pumpkin Seeds
½ Cup	¼ Cup	Wheat Germ

Cereal and Fruit (Mix with dry ingredients):

Full Batch	Half Batch	
1 Cup	½ Cup	Crisp Rice Cereal
½ Cup	¼ Cup	Golden Raisins
1 Cup	½ Cup	Cream-filled Chocolate
(about 12 cookies)	(about 6 cookies)	Cookies (chopped)

Wet Ingredients (<u>Caution</u>: Syrup is very hot! Melt in saucepan until thick, cool slightly, add to mix):

Full Batch	Half Batch	
1 Tablespoon	1 ½ Teaspoons	Butter
¼ Cup	2 Tablespoons	Brown Sugar
¼ Cup	2 Tablespoons	Honey
¼ Cup	2 Tablespoons	Maple Syrup
2 Teaspoons	1 Teaspoon	Vanilla Extract

Candy (Add to mix <u>after</u> wet ingredients have been mixed in):

Full Batch	Half Batch	
¼ Cup	2 Tablespoons	White Chocolate Chips

Spread evenly in pan; bake at 300°F for 25 minutes.

If you would like a different dried fruit in this granola, try ½ cup (¼ cup) of dried papaya (chopped).

Fig Cookie

Dry Ingredients (Bake at 300°F for 10 minutes):

Full Batch	Half Batch	
1 Cup	½ Cup	Old Fashioned Oats
1 Cup	½ Cup	Pecans
½ Cup	¼ Cup	Sunflower Seeds
½ Cup	¼ Cup	Wheat Germ

Cereal and Fruit (Mix with dry ingredients):

Full Batch	Half Batch	
1 Cup	½ Cup	Crisp Rice Cereal
1 Cup	½ Cup	Fig Filled Cookies (chopped)

Wet Ingredients (Melt in saucepan until thick):

Full Batch	Half Batch	
1 Tablespoon	1 ½ Teaspoons	Butter
¼ Cup	2 Tablespoons	Brown Sugar
¼ Cup	2 Tablespoons	Honey
¼ Cup	2 Tablespoons	Maple Syrup
2 Teaspoons	1 Teaspoon	Vanilla Extract

Caution: Syrup is very hot!

Mix wet ingredients with other ingredients, spread evenly in pan; bake at 300°F for 25 minutes.

Made from a cookie that is more like fruit and cake, the soft, sweet texture of the cookie is a fantastic substitute for dried fruit in this granola.

Fruity Nut

Dry Ingredients (Bake at 300°F for 10 minutes):

Full Batch	Half Batch	
1 Cup	½ Cup	Old Fashioned Oats
1 Cup	½ Cup	Cashews
½ Cup	¼ Cup	Sunflower Seeds
½ Cup	¼ Cup	Wheat Germ

Cereal and Fruit (Mix with dry ingredients):

Full Batch	Half Batch	
½ Cup	¼ Cup	Crisp Rice Cereal
1 Cup	½ Cup	Fruity Rice Cereal
1 Cup	½ Cup	Dried Papaya (chopped)

Wet Ingredients (Melt in saucepan until thick):

Full Batch	Half Batch	
1 Tablespoon	1 ½ Teaspoons	Butter
¼ Cup	2 Tablespoons	Brown Sugar
¼ Cup	2 Tablespoons	Honey
¼ Cup	2 Tablespoons	Maple Syrup
2 Teaspoons	1 Teaspoon	Vanilla Extract

Caution: Syrup is very hot!

Mix wet ingredients with other ingredients, spread evenly in pan; bake at 300°F for 25 minutes.

You will enjoy the fruity flavors of the sweet cereal in this granola. You can substitute fruity loop cereal for the fruity rice cereal if desired.

For a chocolatey variation of this granola, try substituting chocolate crisp rice cereal for the plain rice cereal.

Ginger Snap

Dry Ingredients (Bake at 300°F for 10 minutes):

Full Batch	Half Batch	
1 Cup	½ Cup	Old Fashioned Oats
1 Cup	½ Cup	Pecans
½ Cup	¼ Cup	Pumpkin Seeds
½ Cup	¼ Cup	Wheat Germ

Cereal and Fruit (Mix with dry ingredients):

Full Batch	Half Batch	
1 Cup	½ Cup	Crisp Rice Cereal
1 Cup	½ Cup	Ginger Snap Cookies
(about 16 cookies)	(about 8 cookies)	(chopped)
1 Cup	½ Cup	Golden Raisins
1 Teaspoon	½ Teaspoon	Ground Cinnamon
1 Teaspoon	½ Teaspoon	Ground Ginger

Wet Ingredients (Melt in saucepan until thick):

Full Batch	Half Batch	
1 Tablespoon	1 ½ Teaspoons	Butter
¼ Cup	2 Tablespoons	Brown Sugar
¼ Cup	2 Tablespoons	Honey
2 Tablespoons	1 Tablespoon	Maple Syrup
2 Tablespoons	1 Tablespoon	Molasses

<u>Caution</u>: Syrup is very hot! Spread evenly in pan and press firmly if the mixture is not sticky; bake at 300°F for 25 minutes.

This spicy granola really lives up to its namesake, particularly since bits of its namesake are scattered throughout it!

Ginger Snaps can be very hard. Put them in a plastic bag then use a heavy jar to roll over the cookies until they are broken into about quarter inch pieces.

Mocha

Dry Ingredients (Bake at 300°F for 10 minutes):

Full Batch	Half Batch	
1 Cup	½ Cup	Old Fashioned Oats
1 Cup	½ Cup	Slivered Almonds
½ Cup	¼ Cup	Pumpkin Seeds
½ Cup	¼ Cup	Wheat Germ

Cereal and Fruit (Mix with dry ingredients):

Full Batch	Half Batch	
1 Cup	½ Cup	Crisp Brown Rice Cereal
1 Cup	½ Cup	Biscotti (chopped)
½ Cup	¼ Cup	Raisins

Wet Ingredients (Melt in saucepan until thick):

Full Batch	Half Batch	
1 Tablespoon	1 ½ Teaspoons	Butter
¼ Cup	2 Tablespoons	Brown Sugar
¼ Cup	2 Tablespoons	Honey
¼ Cup	2 Tablespoons	Maple Syrup
2 Tablespoons	1 Tablespoon	Instant Coffee Granules
4 Teaspoons	2 Teaspoons	Powdered Milk
2 Tablespoons	1 Tablespoon	Unsweetened Cocoa
1 Teaspoon	½ Teaspoon	Almond Extract
1 Teaspoon	½ Teaspoon	Vanilla Extract

Caution: Syrup is very hot! Mix wet ingredients with other ingredients, spread evenly in pan; bake at 300°F for 25 minutes.

The biscotti cookies add a nice crunch and they are as welcome to a hunk of mocha granola as they are to a mug of mocha java.

Make sure to use instant coffee granules that taste good when they are made into coffee so they will taste good in this granola!

Neapolitan

Dry Ingredients (Bake at 300°F for 10 minutes):

Full Batch	Half Batch	
1 Cup	½ Cup	Old Fashioned Oats
1 Cup	½ Cup	Slivered Almonds
½ Cup	¼ Cup	Pumpkin Seeds
½ Cup	¼ Cup	Wheat Germ

Cereal and Fruit (Mix with dry ingredients):

Full Batch	Half Batch	
1 Cup	½ Cup	Crisp Rice Cereal
1 Cup	½ Cup	Waffle Cones (broken)
½ Cup	¼ Cup	Golden Raisins

Wet Ingredients (<u>Caution</u>: Syrup is very hot! Melt in saucepan until thick, cool slightly, add to mix):

Full Batch	Half Batch	
1 Tablespoon	1 ½ Teaspoons	Butter
¼ Cup	2 Tablespoons	Brown Sugar
2 Tablespoons	1 Tablespoon	Honey
½ Cup	¼ Cup	Strawberry Jam
2 Teaspoons	1 Teaspoon	Vanilla Extract

Candy (Add to mix <u>after</u> wet ingredients have been mixed in):

Full Batch	Half Batch	
¼ Cup	2 Tablespoons	Semi-sweet Chocolate Chips
¼ Cup	2 Tablespoons	White Chocolate Chips

Spread evenly in pan and press firmly; bake at 300°F for 25 minutes.

The classic flavors of Neapolitan ice-cream are in this granola – Chocolate, Vanilla, and Strawberry!

Orange Vanilla

Dry Ingredients (Bake at 300°F for 10 minutes):

Full Batch	Half Batch	
1 Cup	½ Cup	Old Fashioned Oats
1 Cup	½ Cup	Slivered Almonds
½ Cup	¼ Cup	Pumpkin Seeds
½ Cup	¼ Cup	Wheat Germ

Cereal and Fruit (Mix with dry ingredients):

Full Batch	Half Batch	
1 Cup	½ Cup	Crisp Rice Cereal
½ Cup	¼ Cup	Golden Raisins

Wet Ingredients (Caution: Syrup is very hot! Melt in saucepan until thick, cool slightly, add to mix):

Full Batch	Half Batch	
1 Tablespoon	1 ½ Teaspoons	Butter
¼ Cup	2 Tablespoons	Brown Sugar
½ Cup	¼ Cup	Orange Marmalade
2 Teaspoons	1 Teaspoon	Vanilla Extract

Candy (Add to mix after wet ingredients have been mixed in):

Full Batch	Half Batch	
1 Cup	½ Cup	White Chocolate Chips

Spread evenly in pan and press firmly; bake at 300°F for 25 minutes.

Orange and vanilla – a combination that evokes memories of a "dreamy" classic frozen treat. This granola will make you feel like you just chased down an ice-cream truck.

Peaches & Cream

Dry Ingredients (Bake at 300°F for 10 minutes):

Full Batch	Half Batch	
1 Cup	½ Cup	Old Fashioned Oats
1 Cup	½ Cup	Cashews
½ Cup	¼ Cup	Pumpkin Seeds
½ Cup	¼ Cup	Wheat Germ

Cereal and Fruit (Mix with dry ingredients):

Full Batch	Half Batch	
1 Cup	½ Cup	Crisp Rice Cereal
1 Cup	½ Cup	Dried Peaches (chopped)

Wet Ingredients (<u>Caution</u>: Syrup is very hot! Melt in saucepan until thick, cool slightly, add to mix):

Full Batch	Half Batch	
1 Tablespoon	1 ½ Teaspoons	Butter
¼ Cup	2 Tablespoons	Brown Sugar
2 Tablespoons	1 Tablespoon	Honey
½ Cup	¼ Cup	Peach Preserves
2 Teaspoons	1 Teaspoon	Powdered Milk
2 Teaspoons	1 Teaspoon	Vanilla Extract

Candy (Add to mix <u>after</u> wet ingredients have been mixed in):

Full Batch	Half Batch	
1 Cup	½ Cup	White Chocolate Chips

Spread evenly in pan and press firmly; bake at 300°F for 25 minutes.

Be sure to cook the wet ingredients until they are thick so the granola isn't mushy, wet, or sticky. Also, chop the dried peaches into small pieces so they will distribute throughout the granola better.

Spumoni

Dry Ingredients (Bake at 300°F for 10 minutes):

Full Batch	Half Batch	
1 Cup	½ Cup	Old Fashioned Oats
2 Cups	1 Cup	Pistachios (unsalted, chopped)
½ Cup	¼ Cup	Wheat Germ

Cereal and Fruit (Mix with dry ingredients):

Full Batch	Half Batch	
1 Cup	½ Cup	Crisp Rice Cereal
1 Cup	½ Cup	Waffle Cones (broken)
½ Cup	¼ Cup	Candied Cherries (Chopped)

Wet Ingredients (Caution: Syrup is very hot! Melt in saucepan until thick, cool slightly, add to mix):

Full Batch	Half Batch	
1 Tablespoon	1 ½ Teaspoons	Butter
¼ Cup	2 Tablespoons	Brown Sugar
2 Tablespoons	1 Tablespoon	Honey
½ Cup	¼ Cup	Cherry Preserves
2 Teaspoons	1 Teaspoon	Vanilla Extract
2 Teaspoons	1 Teaspoon	Almond Extract

Candy (Add to mix after wet ingredients have been mixed in):

Full Batch	Half Batch	
½ Cup	¼ Cup	Semi-sweet Chocolate Chips

Spread evenly in pan and press firmly if the mixture is not sticky; bake at 300°F for 25 minutes.

Spumoni ice-cream is chocolate, pistachio, and cherry. This granola combines those same flavors (plus the cone!) into perhaps the crunchiest spumoni snack ever!

Vanilla

Dry Ingredients (Bake at 300°F for 10 minutes):

Full Batch	Half Batch	
1 Cup	½ Cup	Old Fashioned Oats
1 Cup	½ Cup	Slivered Almonds
½ Cup	¼ Cup	Sunflower Seeds
½ Cup	¼ Cup	Wheat Germ

Cereal and Fruit (Mix with dry ingredients):

Full Batch	Half Batch	
1 Cup	½ Cup	Crisp Rice Cereal
1 Cup	½ Cup	Vanilla Wafers (chopped)

Wet Ingredients (Caution: Syrup is very hot! Melt in saucepan until thick, cool slightly, add to mix):

Full Batch	Half Batch	
1 Tablespoon	1 ½ Teaspoons	Butter
¼ Cup	2 Tablespoons	Brown Sugar
¼ Cup	2 Tablespoons	Honey
¼ Cup	2 Tablespoons	Maple Syrup
2 Teaspoons	1 Teaspoon	Vanilla Extract

Candy (Add to mix _after_ wet ingredients have been mixed in):

Full Batch	Half Batch	
½ Cup	¼ Cup	Vanilla Yogurt Raisins
½ Cup	¼ Cup	White Chocolate Chips

Spread evenly in pan; bake at 300°F for 25 minutes.

A very vanilla granola. As with other granolas that contain chocolate chips, this granola is not suited to warm conditions because the chocolate can melt and make a big mess – yummy, but messy!

Chapter 3 – Really Weird

The variations of granola in Chapter 1 and in Chapter 2 may be a little unexpected, but still fall within the realm of normalcy.

The variations in this chapter though, are beyond normal. They are very different, very unexpected, but also very good!

Anise

Dry Ingredients (Bake at 300°F for 10 minutes):

Full Batch	Half Batch	
1 Cup	½ Cup	Old Fashioned Oats
1 Cup	½ Cup	Slivered Almonds
½ Cup	¼ Cup	Pumpkin Seeds
½ Cup	¼ Cup	Wheat Germ

Cereal and Fruit (Mix with dry ingredients):

Full Batch	Half Batch	
1 Cup	½ Cup	Crisp Rice Cereal
1 Cup	½ Cup	Raisins

Wet Ingredients (Melt in saucepan until thick):

Full Batch	Half Batch	
1 Tablespoon	1 ½ Teaspoons	Butter
¼ Cup	2 Tablespoons	Brown Sugar
¼ Cup	2 Tablespoons	Honey
¼ Cup	2 Tablespoons	Maple Syrup
1 Teaspoon	½ Teaspoon	Vanilla Extract
2 Teaspoons	1 Teaspoon	Anise Extract

<u>Caution</u>: **Syrup is very hot!**

Mix wet ingredients with other ingredients, spread evenly in pan; bake at 300°F for 25 minutes.

Anise has a mild licorice flavor so it is a little unexpected in granola, but it certainly makes for an oddly delicious granola.

Baklava

Special Ingredient (Bake at 300°F for 20 minutes):

Full Batch	Half Batch	
1 Cup	½ Cup	Filo Dough (See * note below)
(approx 8 sheets)	(approx 4 sheets)	

Dry Ingredients (Bake at 300°F for 10 minutes):

Full Batch	Half Batch	
1 Cup	½ Cup	Old Fashioned Oats
1 Cup	½ Cup	Pistachios (unsalted, chopped)
½ Cup	¼ Cup	Slivered Almonds
½ Cup	¼ Cup	Wheat Germ

Cereal and Fruit (Mix with special ingredient and dry ingredients):

Full Batch	Half Batch	
1 Cup	½ Cup	Crisp Rice Cereal
½ Cup	¼ Cup	Golden Raisins
½ Teaspoon	¼ Teaspoon	Lemon Zest
¼ Teaspoon	1/8 Teaspoon	Ground Cinnamon

Wet Ingredients (Melt in saucepan until thick):

Full Batch	Half Batch	
1 Tablespoon	1 ½ Teaspoons	Butter
¼ Cup	2 Tablespoons	Brown Sugar
½ Cup	¼ Cup	Honey

Caution: Syrup is very hot! Mix wet ingredients with other ingredients, spread evenly in pan; bake at 300°F for 25 minutes.

* See page 78 for instructions for preparing the filo.
Chop the pistachios very small as is customary with traditional baklava.

Boston Baked Beans

Dry Ingredients (Bake at 300°F for 10 minutes):

Full Batch	Half Batch	
1 Cup	½ Cup	Old Fashioned Oats
1 Cup	½ Cup	Peanuts (Unsalted)
½ Cup	¼ Cup	Sunflower Seeds
½ Cup	¼ Cup	Wheat Germ

Cereal and Fruit (Mix with dry ingredients):

Full Batch	Half Batch	
1 Cup	½ Cup	Crisp Rice Cereal
½ Cup	¼ Cup	Bacon (cooked & crumbled)
1 Cup	½ Cup	Raisins

Wet Ingredients (<u>Caution</u>: Syrup is very hot! Melt in saucepan until thick, cool slightly, add to mix):

Full Batch	Half Batch	
1 Tablespoon	1 ½ Teaspoons	Butter
¼ Cup	2 Tablespoons	Brown Sugar
2 Teaspoons	1 Teaspoon	Molasses
½ Cup	¼ Cup	Maple Syrup
2 Teaspoons	1 Teaspoon	Vanilla Extract

Candy (Add to mix <u>after</u> wet ingredients have been mixed in):

Full Batch	Half Batch	
1 Cup	½ Cup	Boston Baked Bean Candies

Spread evenly in pan; bake at 300°F for 25 minutes.

Bacon adds a salty smokiness to this unusual granola. If you have trouble finding Boston Baked Bean candies, look in drugstores, movie theaters, and on the internet.

Caramel Corn

Dry Ingredients (Bake at 300°F for 10 minutes):

Full Batch	Half Batch	
1 Cup	½ Cup	Old Fashioned Oats
1 Cup	½ Cup	Pecans
½ Cup	¼ Cup	Pumpkin Seeds
½ Cup	¼ Cup	Wheat Germ

Cereal and Fruit (Mix with dry ingredients):

Full Batch	Half Batch	
1 Cup	½ Cup	Crisp Brown Rice Cereal
1 ½ Cups	¾ Cup	Popcorn (popped and salted)
1 Cup	½ Cup	Raisins

Wet Ingredients (Melt in saucepan until thick):

Full Batch	Half Batch	
1 Tablespoon	1 ½ Teaspoons	Butter
¼ Cup	2 Tablespoons	Brown Sugar
¼ Cup	2 Tablespoons	Honey
¼ Cup	2 Tablespoons	Maple Syrup
2 Teaspoons	1 Teaspoon	Vanilla Extract

<u>Caution</u>: Syrup is very hot!

Mix wet ingredients with other ingredients, spread evenly in pan; bake at 300°F for 25 minutes.

Put the popcorn into a plastic bag and break it up a bit before you measure it. The smaller pieces distribute throughout the granola better.

Also, Make sure all un-popped kernels are removed before you add the popcorn so there won't be any unpleasant surprises!

Chinese Five Spice

Dry Ingredients (Bake at 300°F for 10 minutes):

Full Batch	Half Batch	
1 Cup	½ Cup	Old Fashioned Oats
½ Cup	¼ Cup	Cashews
½ Cup	¼ Cup	Walnuts
½ Cup	¼ Cup	Sunflower Seeds
½ Cup	¼ Cup	Wheat Germ

Cereal and Fruit (Mix with dry ingredients):

Full Batch	Half Batch	
1 Cup	½ Cup	Crisp Brown Rice Cereal
1 Cup	½ Cup	Raisins
1 Teaspoon	½ Teaspoon	Chinese Five Spice

Wet Ingredients (Melt in saucepan until thick):

Full Batch	Half Batch	
1 Tablespoon	1 ½ Teaspoons	Butter
¼ Cup	2 Tablespoons	Brown Sugar
¼ Cup	2 Tablespoons	Honey
¼ Cup	2 Tablespoons	Maple Syrup
1 Teaspoon	½ Teaspoon	Vanilla Extract

<u>Caution</u>: Syrup is very hot!

Mix wet ingredients with other ingredients, spread evenly in pan; bake at 300°F for 25 minutes.

The five spices in Chinese Five Spice seasoning are anise, cinnamon, star anise, clove, and ginger. The exotic flavors of the five spice seasoning blend beautifully with the cashews, walnuts, and raisins.

Coffee Bean

Dry Ingredients (Bake at 300°F for 10 minutes):

Full Batch	Half Batch	
1 Cup	½ Cup	Old Fashioned Oats
1 Cup	½ Cup	Slivered Almonds
½ Cup	¼ Cup	Pumpkin Seeds
½ Cup	¼ Cup	Wheat Germ

Cereal and Fruit (Mix with dry ingredients):

Full Batch	Half Batch	
1 Cup	½ Cup	Crisp Brown Rice Cereal
1 Cup	½ Cup	Golden Raisins

Wet Ingredients (<u>Caution</u>: Syrup is very hot! Melt in saucepan until thick, cool slightly, add to mix):

Full Batch	Half Batch	
1 Tablespoon	1 ½ Teaspoons	Butter
¼ Cup	2 Tablespoons	Brown Sugar
½ Cup	¼ Cup	Maple Syrup
1 Teaspoon	½ Teaspoon	Vanilla Extract

Candy (Add to mix <u>after</u> wet ingredients have been mixed in):

Full Batch	Half Batch	
½ Cup	¼ Cup	Coffee Beans
½ Cup	¼ Cup	Semi-sweet Chocolate Chips
	--OR--	
1 Cup	½ Cup	Chocolate Covered Coffee Beans

Spread evenly in pan; bake at 300°F for 25 minutes.

Use coffee beans you enjoy as brewed coffee because if you don't enjoy them brewed, you probably won't enjoy them in granola!

Honey Mustard

Dry Ingredients (Bake at 300°F for 10 minutes):

Full Batch	Half Batch	
1 Cup	½ Cup	Old Fashioned Oats
¼ Cup	2 Tablespoons	Slivered Almonds
¼ Cup	2 Tablespoons	Cashews
¼ Cup	2 Tablespoons	Peanuts (unsalted)
¼ Cup	2 Tablespoons	Walnuts
½ Cup	¼ Cup	Pumpkin Seeds
½ Cup	¼ Cup	Wheat Germ

Cereal and Fruit (Mix with dry ingredients):

Full Batch	Half Batch	
1 Cup	½ Cup	Crisp Brown Rice Cereal
1 Cup	½ Cup	Raisins

Wet Ingredients (Melt in saucepan until thick):

Full Batch	Half Batch	
1 Tablespoon	1 ½ Teaspoons	Butter
¼ Cup	2 Tablespoons	Brown Sugar
½ Cup	¼ Cup	Honey
¼ Cup	2 Tablespoons	Dijon Mustard
2 Teaspoons	1 Teaspoon	Vanilla Extract

<u>Caution</u>: **Syrup is very hot!**

Mix wet ingredients with other ingredients, spread evenly in pan and press firmly; bake at 300°F for 25 minutes.

Though it may seem a little strange at first, the mustard complements the sweetness of the honey and the earthiness of the mixed nuts. It adds a subtle, unexpected spiciness to this unusual granola.

Ketchup

Dry Ingredients (Bake at 300°F for 10 minutes):

Full Batch	Half Batch	
1 Cup	½ Cup	Old Fashioned Oats
1 Cup	½ Cup	Cashews
½ Cup	¼ Cup	Pumpkin Seeds
½ Cup	¼ Cup	Wheat Germ

Cereal and Fruit (Mix with dry ingredients):

Full Batch	Half Batch	
1 Cup	½ Cup	Crisp Rice Cereal
1 Cup	½ Cup	Sun-dried Tomatoes (Chopped)

Wet Ingredients (Melt in saucepan until thick):

Full Batch	Half Batch	
1 Tablespoon	1 ½ Teaspoons	Butter
¼ Cup	2 Tablespoons	Brown Sugar
¼ Cup	2 Tablespoons	Honey
¼ Cup	2 Tablespoons	Ketchup

<u>Caution</u>: Syrup is very hot!

Mix wet ingredients with other ingredients, spread evenly in pan and press firmly; bake at 300°F for 25 minutes.

Though we generally think of ketchup as a savory seasoning, it is actually quite sweet. The mild flavor of cashews and the addition of sun-dried tomatoes help the tomato flavor of this very unusual granola shine through.

If the sun-dried tomatoes are hard, soften them per the instructions accompanying them or put them in a bowl of boiling water for about 5 minutes, then pat them dry before chopping them.

Mojito

Dry Ingredients (Bake at 300°F for 10 minutes):

Full Batch	Half Batch	
1 Cup	½ Cup	Old Fashioned Oats
1 Cup	½ Cup	Slivered Almonds
½ Cup	¼ Cup	Pumpkin Seeds
½ Cup	¼ Cup	Wheat Germ

Cereal and Fruit (Mix with dry ingredients):

Full Batch	Half Batch	
1 Cup	½ Cup	Crisp Rice Cereal
2 Teaspoons	1 Teaspoon	Lime Zest
1 Cup	½ Cup	Golden Raisins

Wet Ingredients (Melt in saucepan until thick):

Full Batch	Half Batch	
1 Tablespoon	1 ½ Teaspoons	Butter
¼ Cup	2 Tablespoons	Brown Sugar
¼ Cup	2 Tablespoons	Honey
¼ Cup	2 Tablespoons	Maple Syrup
½ Teaspoon	¼ Teaspoon	Peppermint Extract
1 Tablespoon	1 ½ Teaspoons	Rum Extract

Caution: Syrup is very hot!

Mix wet ingredients with other ingredients, spread evenly in pan; bake at 300°F for 25 minutes.

A Mojito (sounds like Moe-hee-toe) is a Cuban drink made with white rum, lime juice, fresh mint, and sparkling water.

Peanut Butter & Cheese Crackers

Dry Ingredients (Bake at 300°F for 10 minutes):

Full Batch	Half Batch	
1 Cup	½ Cup	Old Fashioned Oats
1 Cup	½ Cup	Peanuts (unsalted)
½ Cup	¼ Cup	Sunflower Seeds
½ Cup	¼ Cup	Wheat Germ

Cereal and Fruit (Mix with dry ingredients):

Full Batch	Half Batch	
1 Cup	½ Cup	Crisp Rice Cereal
1 Cup	½ Cup	Cheese Crackers (broken)
1 Cup	½ Cup	Golden Raisins

Wet Ingredients (Melt in saucepan until thick):

Full Batch	Half Batch	
1 Tablespoon	1 ½ Teaspoons	Butter
¼ Cup	2 Tablespoons	Brown Sugar
¼ Cup	2 Tablespoons	Honey
¼ Cup	2 Tablespoons	Maple Syrup
2 Tablespoons	1 Tablespoon	Peanut Butter (at end)
2 Teaspoons	1 Teaspoon	Vanilla Extract

<u>Caution</u>: Syrup is very hot!

Mix wet ingredients with other ingredients, spread evenly in pan; bake at 300°F for 25 minutes.

Add the peanut butter at the end of the cooking process, just before you combine the wet ingredients to the dry ingredients.

Peanut butter and cheese seems like a strange combination, but little sandwiches made of peanut butter and cheese crackers are a popular snack. This granola brings that popular snack into a whole new realm!

Peanut Butter & Jelly

Dry Ingredients (Bake at 300°F for 10 minutes):

Full Batch	Half Batch	
1 Cup	½ Cup	Old Fashioned Oats
½ Cup	¼ Cup	Peanuts (unsalted)
½ Cup	¼ Cup	Sunflower Seeds
½ Cup	¼ Cup	Wheat Germ

Cereal and Fruit (Mix with dry ingredients):

Full Batch	Half Batch	
1 Cup	½ Cup	Crisp Brown Rice Cereal

Wet Ingredients (<u>Caution</u>: Syrup is very hot! Melt in saucepan until thick, cool slightly, add to mix):

Full Batch	Half Batch	
1 Tablespoon	1 ½ Teaspoons	Butter
¼ Cup	2 Tablespoons	Brown Sugar
¼ Cup	2 Tablespoons	Maple Syrup
1 Teaspoon	½ Teaspoon	Vanilla Extract

Candy (Add to mix <u>after</u> wet ingredients have been mixed in):

Full Batch	Half Batch	
½ Cup	¼ Cup	Candy Coated Peanut Butter
½ Cup	¼ Cup	Grape Jelly Beans –or– Gum Drops

Spread evenly in pan; bake at 300°F for 25 minutes.

Peanut butter chips (like chocolate chips) can be used instead of the candy coated peanut butter. Also, some jelly beans are already very small, but if yours are not or you if are using gum drops, cut them into small pieces before measuring and adding them. This granola is best at room temperature.

Pretzel

Dry Ingredients (Bake at 300°F for 10 minutes):

Full Batch	Half Batch	
1 Cup	½ Cup	Old Fashioned Oats
1 Cup	½ Cup	Pecans
½ Cup	¼ Cup	Pumpkin Seeds
½ Cup	¼ Cup	Wheat Germ

Cereal and Fruit (Mix with dry ingredients):

Full Batch	Half Batch	
1 Cup	½ Cup	Crisp Brown Rice Cereal
1 Cup	½ Cup	Pretzels (broken)
1 Cup	½ Cup	Golden Raisins

Wet Ingredients (<u>Caution</u>: Syrup is very hot! Melt in saucepan until thick, cool slightly, add to mix):

Full Batch	Half Batch	
1 Tablespoon	1 ½ Teaspoons	Butter
¼ Cup	2 Tablespoons	Brown Sugar
¼ Cup	2 Tablespoons	Honey
¼ Cup	2 Tablespoons	Maple Syrup
2 Teaspoons	1 Teaspoon	Vanilla Extract

Candy (Add to mix <u>after</u> wet ingredients have been mixed in):

Full Batch	Half Batch	
½ Cup	¼ Cup	White Chocolate Chips

Spread evenly in pan; bake at 300°F for 25 minutes.

The saltiness of the pretzels contrasts well with the sweetness of the raisins and whit chocolate.

Root Beer Float

Dry Ingredients (Bake at 300°F for 10 minutes):

Full Batch	Half Batch	
1 Cup	½ Cup	Old Fashioned Oats
1 Cup	½ Cup	Pecans
½ Cup	¼ Cup	Pumpkin Seeds
½ Cup	¼ Cup	Wheat Germ

Cereal and Fruit (Mix with dry ingredients):

Full Batch	Half Batch	
1 Cup	½ Cup	Crisp Rice Cereal
½ Cup	¼ Cup	Golden Raisins

Wet Ingredients (<u>Caution</u>: Syrup is very hot! Melt in saucepan until thick, cool slightly, add to mix):

Full Batch	Half Batch	
1 Tablespoon	1 ½ Teaspoons	Butter
¼ Cup	2 Tablespoons	Brown Sugar
¼ Cup	2 Tablespoons	Honey
¼ Cup	2 Tablespoons	Maple Syrup
1 Teaspoon	½ Teaspoon	Vanilla Extract
½ Teaspoon	¼ Teaspoon	Root Beer Concentrate

Candy (Add to mix <u>after</u> wet ingredients have been mixed in):

Full Batch	Half Batch	
½ Cup	¼ Cup	White Chocolate Chips

Spread evenly in pan; bake at 300°F for 25 minutes.

Since root beer concentrate is not an extract, it is very strong and only a small amount is needed to flavor this granola. The white chocolate chips substitute for the vanilla ice-cream in a traditional root beer float, so this granola is almost as much a treat as its namesake!

Rosemary

Dry Ingredients (Bake at 300°F for 10 minutes):

Full Batch	Half Batch	
1 Cup	½ Cup	Old Fashioned Oats
1 Cup	½ Cup	Pecans
½ Cup	¼ Cup	Pumpkin Seeds
½ Cup	¼ Cup	Wheat Germ

Cereal and Fruit (Mix with dry ingredients):

Full Batch	Half Batch	
1 Cup	½ Cup	Crisp Rice Cereal
1 Cup	½ Cup	Golden Raisins
½ Teaspoon	¼ Teaspoon	Ground Cinnamon
¼ Teaspoon	1/8 Teaspoon	Ground Nutmeg
1 Teaspoon	½ Teaspoon	Lemon Zest
2 Teaspoons	1 Teaspoon	Fresh Rosemary (chopped finely)

Wet Ingredients (Melt in saucepan until thick):

Full Batch	Half Batch	
1 Tablespoon	1 ½ Teaspoons	Butter
¼ Cup	2 Tablespoons	Brown Sugar
¼ Cup	2 Tablespoons	Honey
¼ Cup	2 Tablespoons	Maple Syrup
1 Teaspoon	½ Teaspoon	Vanilla Extract

<u>Caution</u>: **Syrup is very hot! Mix wet ingredients with other ingredients, spread evenly in pan; bake at 300°F for 25 minutes.**

Rosemary may seem like an odd flavoring for a sweet granola since it is normally used in savory dishes, but in Europe it is not unusual to see rosemary in cookies. The hint of cinnamon, nutmeg, and lemon help bring out the essence of the rosemary and the pecans complement all of the flavors especially well.

Rum Raisin

Dry Ingredients (Bake at 300°F for 10 minutes):

Full Batch	Half Batch	
1 Cup	½ Cup	Old Fashioned Oats
1 Cup	½ Cup	Pecans
½ Cup	¼ Cup	Pumpkin Seeds
½ Cup	¼ Cup	Wheat Germ

Cereal and Fruit (Mix with dry ingredients):

Full Batch	Half Batch	
1 Cup	½ Cup	Crisp Rice Cereal
1 Cup	½ Cup	Raisins

Wet Ingredients (Melt in saucepan until thick):

Full Batch	Half Batch	
1 Tablespoon	1 ½ Teaspoons	Butter
¼ Cup	2 Tablespoons	Brown Sugar
¼ Cup	2 Tablespoons	Honey
¼ Cup	2 Tablespoons	Maple Syrup
1 Teaspoon	½ Teaspoon	Vanilla Extract
2 Teaspoons	1 Teaspoon	Rum Extract

<u>Caution</u>: **Syrup is very hot!**

Mix wet ingredients with other ingredients, spread evenly in pan; bake at 300°F for 25 minutes.

This granola is more delicately flavored than you might think. The rum extract adds interesting notes and complements the raisins wonderfully.

Chapter 4 – Celebrations

These granola recipes welcome holidays and special occasions. They make great gifts as well as wonderful party and pot-luck snacks!

Ball Game

Dry Ingredients (Bake at 300°F for 10 minutes):

Full Batch	Half Batch	
1 Cup	½ Cup	Old Fashioned Oats
1 Cup	½ Cup	Peanuts (Salted)
½ Cup	¼ Cup	Sunflower Seeds
½ Cup	¼ Cup	Wheat Germ

Cereal and Fruit (Mix with dry ingredients):

Full Batch	Half Batch	
1 Cup	½ Cup	Crisp Rice Cereal
4 Cups	2 Cups	Candied Popcorn & Peanuts
1 Cup	½ Cup	Raisins

Wet Ingredients (Melt in saucepan until thick):

Full Batch	Half Batch	
1 Tablespoon	1 ½ Teaspoons	Butter
¼ Cup	2 Tablespoons	Brown Sugar
¼ Cup	2 Tablespoons	Honey
¼ Cup	2 Tablespoons	Maple Syrup
2 Teaspoons	1 Teaspoon	Vanilla Extract

<u>Caution</u>: Syrup is very hot!

Mix wet ingredients with other ingredients, spread evenly in pan; bake at 300°F for 25 minutes.

Bake me up some granola! Bake me up a whole pan!
Throw in some peanuts and Cracker Jacks,
I think now it's my favorite snack!
Let me munch, munch, munch on granola,
If it gets burned it's a shame!
Cuz its 1, 2, 3 minutes 'til the one called Ball Game!

Birthday Cake

Dry Ingredients (Bake at 300°F for 10 minutes):

Full Batch	Half Batch	
1 Cup	½ Cup	Old Fashioned Oats
1 Cup	½ Cup	Slivered Almonds
½ Cup	¼ Cup	Pumpkin Seeds
½ Cup	¼ Cup	Wheat Germ

Cereal and Fruit (Mix with dry ingredients):

Full Batch	Half Batch	
1 Cup	½ Cup	Crisp Rice Cereal
2 Cups (about 4 cakes)	1 Cup (about 2 cakes)	Cream Filled Vanilla Snack Cakes (chopped small)
1 Cup	½ Cup	Golden Raisins

Wet Ingredients (<u>Caution</u>: Syrup is very hot! Melt in saucepan until thick, cool slightly, add to mix):

Full Batch	Half Batch	
1 Tablespoon	1 ½ Teaspoons	Butter
¼ Cup	2 Tablespoons	Brown Sugar
¼ Cup	2 Tablespoons	Honey
¼ Cup	2 Tablespoons	Maple Syrup
2 Teaspoons	1 Teaspoon	Vanilla Extract

Candy (Add to mix <u>after</u> wet ingredients have been mixed in):

Full Batch	Half Batch	
½ Cup	¼ Cup	Sprinkles (<u>not</u> nonpareil)
½ Cup	¼ Cup	White Chocolate Chips

Spread evenly in pan and press firmly; bake at 300°F for 25 minutes.

Happy Birthday to you!!!

Campfire S'Mores

Dry Ingredients (Bake at 300°F for 10 minutes):

Full Batch	Half Batch	
1 Cup	½ Cup	Old Fashioned Oats
1 Cup	½ Cup	Pecans
½ Cup	¼ Cup	Pumpkin Seeds
½ Cup	¼ Cup	Wheat Germ

Cereal and Fruit (Mix with dry ingredients):

Full Batch	Half Batch	
½ Cup	¼ Cup	Crisp Rice Cereal
1 Cup	½ Cup	Graham Crackers (broken)
½ Cup	¼ Cup	Golden Raisins

Wet Ingredients (<u>Caution</u>: Syrup is very hot! Melt in saucepan until thick, cool slightly, add to mix):

Full Batch	Half Batch	
1 Tablespoon	1 ½ Teaspoons	Butter
¼ Cup	2 Tablespoons	Brown Sugar
¼ Cup	2 Tablespoons	Honey
¼ Cup	2 Tablespoons	Maple Syrup
2 Teaspoons	1 Teaspoon	Vanilla Extract

Candy (Add to mix <u>after</u> wet ingredients have been mixed in):

Full Batch	Half Batch	
½ Cup	¼ Cup	Semi-sweet Chocolate Chips
½ Cup	¼ Cup	Miniature Marshmallows

Spread evenly in pan; bake at 300°F for 25 minutes.

For a special treat, try this granola while it is still warm! It is better served at room temperature. For an extra treat, sprinkle some marshmallows over the top in the last 10 minutes of baking.

Candy Corn

Dry Ingredients (Bake at 300°F for 10 minutes):

Full Batch	Half Batch	
1 Cup	½ Cup	Old Fashioned Oats
1 Cup	½ Cup	Pecans
½ Cup	¼ Cup	Pumpkin Seeds
½ Cup	¼ Cup	Wheat Germ

Cereal and Fruit (Mix with dry ingredients):

Full Batch	Half Batch	
1 Cup	½ Cup	Crisp Brown Rice Cereal
1 Cup	½ Cup	Corn Flake Cereal
1 Cup	½ Cup	Golden Raisins

Wet Ingredients (<u>Caution</u>: Syrup is very hot! Melt in saucepan until thick, cool slightly, add to mix):

Full Batch	Half Batch	
1 Tablespoon	1 ½ Teaspoons	Butter
¼ Cup	2 Tablespoons	Brown Sugar
¼ Cup	2 Tablespoons	Honey
¼ Cup	2 Tablespoons	Maple Syrup
2 Teaspoons	1 Teaspoon	Vanilla Extract

Spread evenly in pan; bake at 300°F for 25 minutes.

Candy (Press onto the top of the granola as it is cooling):

Full Batch	Half Batch	
1 Cup	½ Cup	Candy Corn (chopped)

What says Fall (or Autumn) better than candy corn?

Figgy Pudding

Dry Ingredients (Bake at 300°F for 10 minutes):

Full Batch	Half Batch	
1 Cup	½ Cup	Old Fashioned Oats
1 Cup	½ Cup	Walnuts
½ Cup	¼ Cup	Pumpkin Seeds
½ Cup	¼ Cup	Wheat Germ

Cereal and Fruit (Mix with dry ingredients):

Full Batch	Half Batch	
1 Cup	½ Cup	Crisp Rice Cereal
1 Cup	½ Cup	Dried Figs (chopped)
1 Teaspoon	½ Teaspoon	Ground Cinnamon
½ Teaspoon	¼ Teaspoon	Ground Nutmeg

Wet Ingredients (Melt in saucepan until thick):

Full Batch	Half Batch	
1 Tablespoon	1 ½ Teaspoons	Butter
¼ Cup	2 Tablespoons	Brown Sugar
½ Cup	¼ Cup	Fig Preserves
1 Teaspoon	½ Teaspoon	Vanilla Extract
2 Teaspoons	1 Teaspoon	Brandy Extract

<u>Caution</u>: **Syrup is very hot!**

Mix wet ingredients with other ingredients, spread evenly in pan and press firmly if the mixture is not sticky; bake at 300°F for 25 minutes.

Figgy pudding is not a milk-based, soft, creamy dessert. In Great Britain, a "pudding" may also be a type of cake. Traditional figgy pudding is a treat normally reserved for after Christmas dinner and takes hours to prepare. It is usually served with a custard sauce flavored with brandy, rum, or cognac.

Fruit Cake

Dry Ingredients (Bake at 300°F for 10 minutes):

Full Batch	Half Batch	
1 Cup	½ Cup	Old Fashioned Oats
1 Cup	½ Cup	Pecans
½ Cup	¼ Cup	Pumpkin Seeds
½ Cup	¼ Cup	Wheat Germ

Cereal and Fruit (Mix with dry ingredients):

Full Batch	Half Batch	
1 Cup	½ Cup	Crisp Rice Cereal
½ Cup	¼ Cup	Raisins
1 Cup	½ Cup	Candied –or– Dried Fruit
2 Teaspoons	1 Teaspoon	Pumpkin Pie Spice

Wet Ingredients (Melt in saucepan until thick):

Full Batch	Half Batch	
1 Tablespoon	1 ½ Teaspoons	Butter
¼ Cup	2 Tablespoons	Brown Sugar
¼ Cup	2 Tablespoons	Honey
2 Tablespoons	1 Tablespoon	Maple Syrup
2 Tablespoons	1 Tablespoon	Orange Marmalade
1 Tablespoon	1 ½ Teaspoons	Molasses
1 Teaspoon	½ Teaspoon	Brandy –or– Rum Extract

<u>Caution</u>: Syrup is very hot! **Spread evenly in pan and press firmly if the mixture is not sticky; bake at 300°F for 25 minutes.**

To imitate the much maligned holiday cake, use green and red candied cherries and candied pineapple. For a more classic imitation, use dried cherries, dried currants, and dried pineapple. Whether you choose doorstop or traditional, be sure to chop the fruits into small pieces so they distribute better throughout the granola.

Hearts Afire

Dry Ingredients (Bake at 300°F for 10 minutes):

Full Batch	Half Batch	
1 Cup	½ Cup	Old Fashioned Oats
1 Cup	½ Cup	Slivered Almonds
½ Cup	¼ Cup	Pumpkin Seeds
½ Cup	¼ Cup	Wheat Germ

Cereal and Fruit (Mix with dry ingredients):

Full Batch	Half Batch	
1 Cup	½ Cup	Crisp Rice Cereal
1 Cup	½ Cup	Golden Raisins

Wet Ingredients (<u>Caution</u>: Syrup is very hot! Melt in saucepan until thick, cool slightly, add to mix):

Full Batch	Half Batch	
1 Tablespoon	1 ½ Teaspoons	Butter
¼ Cup	2 Tablespoons	Brown Sugar
¼ Cup	2 Tablespoons	Honey
¼ Cup	2 Tablespoons	Maple Syrup
2 Teaspoons	1 Teaspoon	Almond Extract

Candy (Add to mix <u>after</u> wet ingredients have been mixed in):

Full Batch	Half Batch	
½ Cup	¼ Cup	Candy Hearts
½ Cup	¼ Cup	Hot Cinnamon Candies

Spread evenly in pan; bake at 300°F for 25 minutes.

For your sweetie!!!

Loaded Diaper

Dry Ingredients (Bake at 300°F for 10 minutes):

Full Batch	Half Batch	
1 Cup	½ Cup	Old Fashioned Oats
1 Cup	½ Cup	Walnuts
½ Cup	¼ Cup	Pumpkin Seeds
½ Cup	¼ Cup	Wheat Germ

Cereal and Fruit (Mix with dry ingredients):

Full Batch	Half Batch	
1 Cup	½ Cup	Crisp Rice Cereal
1 Cup	½ Cup	Golden Raisins
2 Teaspoons	1 Teaspoon	Lemon Zest
2 Cups	1 Cup	Fudge Brownies (chopped)

Wet Ingredients (Melt in saucepan until thick):

Full Batch	Half Batch	
1 Tablespoon	1 ½ Teaspoons	Butter
¼ Cup	2 Tablespoons	Brown Sugar
¼ Cup	2 Tablespoons	Honey
¼ Cup	2 Tablespoons	Maple Syrup
2 Teaspoons	1 Teaspoon	Vanilla Extract

<u>Caution</u>: Syrup is very hot!

Mix wet ingredients with other ingredients, spread evenly in pan; bake at 300°F for 25 minutes.

This granola is named for a cake I once made for a baby shower. I made it with chocolate butter cream between the bottom layer and middle layer and lemon curd between the middle layer and the top layer. Despite its silly name, this granola is truly delicious and will be a hit at any baby shower!

Mincemeat Pie

Dry Ingredients (Bake at 300°F for 10 minutes):

Full Batch	Half Batch	
1 Cup	½ Cup	Old Fashioned Oats
1 Cup	½ Cup	Pecans
½ Cup	¼ Cup	Pumpkin Seeds
½ Cup	¼ Cup	Wheat Germ

Cereal and Fruit (Mix with dry ingredients):

Full Batch	Half Batch	
1 Cup	½ Cup	Crisp Rice Cereal
2 Teaspoons	1 Teaspoon	Lemon Zest
2 Teaspoons	1 Teaspoon	Orange Zest
1 Cup	½ Cup	Animal Crackers (chopped)

Wet Ingredients (Melt in saucepan until thick – <u>Caution</u>: Syrup is very hot!):

Full Batch	Half Batch	
1 Tablespoon	1 ½ Teaspoons	Butter
¼ Cup	2 Tablespoons	Brown Sugar
¼ Cup	2 Tablespoons	Honey
1 Cup	½ Cup	Mincemeat
2 Teaspoons	1 Teaspoon	Brandy Extract

Mix wet ingredients with other ingredients, spread evenly in pan and press firmly if the mixture is not sticky; bake at 300°F for 25 minutes.

Mincemeat does not always contain any meat, though it may contain beef suet or lard. Mincemeat pies and tarts are often served as a popular holiday treat for Christmas and the New Year. The animal crackers in this granola substitute for the pie crust, though if you have some leftover pie dough, bake it and cut it into small pieces then replace the animal crackers with real pie crust.

Red, White, and Blue

Dry Ingredients (Bake at 300°F for 10 minutes):

Full Batch	Half Batch	
1 Cup	½ Cup	Old Fashioned Oats
1 Cup	½ Cup	Pecans
½ Cup	¼ Cup	Pumpkin Seeds
½ Cup	¼ Cup	Wheat Germ

Cereal and Fruit (Mix with dry ingredients):

Full Batch	Half Batch	
1 Cup	½ Cup	Crisp Brown Rice Cereal
1 Cup	½ Cup	Dried Blueberries
1 Cup	½ Cup	Dried Cranberries

Wet Ingredients (<u>Caution</u>: Syrup is very hot! Melt in saucepan until thick, cool slightly, add to mix):

Full Batch	Half Batch	
1 Tablespoon	1 ½ Teaspoons	Butter
¼ Cup	2 Tablespoons	Brown Sugar
¼ Cup	2 Tablespoons	Honey
¼ Cup	2 Tablespoons	Maple Syrup
2 Teaspoons	1 Teaspoon	Vanilla Extract

Candy (Add to mix <u>after</u> wet ingredients have been mixed in):

Full Batch	Half Batch	
½ Cup	¼ Cup	White Chocolate Chips

Spread evenly in pan; bake at 300°F for 25 minutes.

<u>Red</u> cranberries, <u>white</u> chocolate chips and <u>blue</u>berries!

Chapter 5 – Notes and Tips

Every recipe in this cookbook was tested to ensure the directions are accurate, ingredients work well with each other, and the overall flavor of the granola is good.

So, from experience, here are some additional notes and tips that will help you get the best results.

Dry Ingredients

♫ Oats

There are various kinds of oats available, but only two kinds of rolled oats are considered for these granola recipes – Old Fashioned Oats and Quick Oats.

When used to make oatmeal, Old Fashioned Oats require a longer cooking time than Quick Oats. Old Fashioned Oats are the better choice for making granola – they are less processed so they hold up better in granola. However, Quick Oats can be used as a substitution if necessary or desired. You may even find a personal preference for granola made with Quick Oats.

It may seem odd to toast the oats, but toasting them brings out a little nuttiness and helps them stand up to the syrupy wet ingredients later.

♫ Nuts

Most of the granola recipes in this book have at least one kind of nut. The nuts add bulk, texture, and flavor and are an important ingredient.

Toasting the nuts helps bring out their flavors, but over-toasting can ruin the flavor. Since the nuts will be baked twice, first to toast them and again once they are incorporated into the granola, don't toast nuts any higher than 300° F and don't toast them longer than 10 minutes.

Most of the recipes do not specify if the nuts should be chopped or left whole. Leaving the nuts whole or chopping them is a personal preference. If you intend to break the granola into fairly large pieces, whole nuts may be okay, but if you want to break the granola into smaller pieces, you may want to chop the nuts. Finely chopped nuts are generally not as good as larger pieces, though.

The nut or nuts chosen for a particular granola were selected based on several criteria. If the nut is to be a prominent flavor, nuts with a relatively strong flavor like walnuts or hazelnuts are used. If the nut is there to complement the other flavors in the granola, nuts with a milder flavor are used like pecans and almonds. The choice of nut may also have been based on textural reasons too.

Most of the recipes use unsalted nuts, but salted nuts can be used and often add an interesting balance to the sweetness of the other ingredients.

You may want to substitute a different nut in a recipe based on your own personal tastes. Most substitutions should not affect the results, but be sure to maintain the same proportions indicated in the recipe. For example, if a recipe calls for ½ cup of walnuts, you may decide to use a combination of hazelnuts and pecans. Just make sure the combined total is still equal to ½ cup.

♪ Seeds

Most of the granola recipes in this book have at least one kind of seed. Like the nuts in the granola, the seeds add bulk, texture, and flavor and are an important ingredient as well.

As with nuts, toasting the seeds helps bring out their flavor, but over-toasting can ruin them too, so don't toast the seeds higher than 300° F and don't toast the seeds for longer than 10 minutes.

There are three different kinds of seeds used in the recipes in this book – pumpkin seeds, sunflower seeds, and sesame seeds. They were chosen for each recipe based on flavor.

Pumpkin seeds have the mildest flavor which makes them perfect as a background ingredient.

Sunflower seeds have a stronger flavor than pumpkin seeds and are used when their flavor is needed to complement the other flavors in the granola.

Sesame seeds have a very distinct, strong flavor. They are used when that strong flavor is desired, particularly in Asian-inspired granolas.

♫ Wheat Germ

Wheat germ adds very little flavor to the granola recipes in this book, but they do add fiber as well as additional texture.

Wheat germ can be found toasted or un-toasted, sweetened or unsweetened. The recipes in this book were tested with pre-toasted, unsweetened wheat germ.

Un-toasted wheat germ should be toasted as directed in the basic recipe – no higher than 300° F and for no longer than 10 minutes.

If you use sweetened wheat germ, don't try to compensate by reducing the brown sugar or other wet ingredients as this may cause problems "gluing" all of the ingredients together.

Cereal and Fruit

♫ Cereal

All of the recipes in this book use some type of crisp rice cereal. The rice cereal helps keep the granola light and gives it a crispier texture.

There are three kinds of crisp rice cereal used in this book – Crisp Brown Rice Cereal, regular Crisp Rice Cereal, and Chocolate Crisp Rice Cereal.

Brown Rice Cereal generally has less sugar than regular crisp rice cereal which is why it is indicated more in the Healthy chapter, but brown rice cereal and plain rice cereal can be used interchangeably.

Chocolate crisp rice cereal is used when a chocolate flavor is desired. Similar results can be obtained by using either brown or plain crisp rice cereal plus 2 teaspoons of unsweetened cocoa powder (1 teaspoon for half batch). If you use cocoa, mix it into the wet ingredients so it will distribute throughout the granola better.

One recipe calls for "Fruity Rice Cereal". You can substitute almost any kind of fruity cereal in that recipe if desired.

A couple of recipes call for "Toasted Oat Cereal". Any kind of toasted oat cereal can be used, even "puffed" oat cereal.

♫ Fruit

Most of the recipes in this book use some kind of dried fruit. Unless the dried fruit is already small, like cranberries and blueberries, it is better to chop it into small pieces so it can distribute throughout the granola more evenly. If the pieces are sticky, rub some wheat germ on the pieces so they don't clump together.

In recipes where **lemon** or **lime** zest is required, use fresh, firm fruit and a fine grater. Grate only the colored part of the skin and not the bitter white part called the pith.

Dried cherries can be quite tart, so if you prefer sweeter cherries use candies cherries, like the kind used in fruit cakes, but not maraschino cherries because they are too wet and can make the granola mushy.

Wet Ingredients

Sometimes jams, jellies, marmalades, preserves, or other wet ingredients like ketchup or mustard are used in place of honey or maple syrup. When these ingredients are used the mixture may not be as sticky as it is in other recipes. Normally it is better not to pack the mixture into the baking pan, but if the mixture does not seem very sticky, it is better to press it into the pan to help it stick together better. The recipe directions indicate if the mixture should be pressed into the pan.

♫ Butter

Margarine can be substituted for the butter in all of the recipes in this book. The butter helps keep the other wet ingredients from sticking the saucepan and it helps keep the granola from sticking to the pan so much.

♫ Brown Sugar

All of the recipes in this book use brown sugar. It is needed to make the syrup that helps bind or "glue" the other ingredients together. Dark brown sugar works the best, but light brown sugar will work too.

♬ Honey

Many of the recipes in this book use honey. Like brown sugar, it helps make the syrup needed to bind or "glue" the other ingredients together. If you prefer the flavor of honey, you can substitute honey for the maple syrup.

♬ Maple Syrup

Many of the recipes in this book use maple syrup. As with brown sugar and honey, tt helps make the syrup needed to bind or "glue" the other ingredients together. If you prefer the flavor of maple, you can substitute maple syrup for the honey.

♬ Jams, Jellies, Marmalades, and Preserves

Some of the recipes in this book use jam, jelly, marmalade, or preserves in place of the honey and/or maple syrup. When any of these are used, be sure the wet ingredients thicken a little before adding them to the dry ingredients.

It is better to use natural or fruit juice sweetened products, but if you cannot find them, use regular versions. Low sugar products **do not** work. These recipes were not tested with products that use artificial sweeteners, so it would be better to avoid them.

Preserves often have large chunks of fruit. Try to smash the large chunks, but if they do not break up into the syrup, remove them before adding the wet ingredients to the dry ingredients.

♬ Peanut Butter

When peanut butter is used you must add it to the wet ingredients at the end of the cooking process, right before you add the wet ingredients to the dry ingredients. Use "natural" peanut butter, i.e. peanut butter made with just peanuts or peanuts and salt, but no other ingredients like sugar or other sweeteners.

♫ Mustard and Ketchup

One of the recipes in this book uses mustard and another uses ketchup. These ingredients are not very sticky, so the syrup must be cooked longer to get a stickier consistency. The ketchup recipe was tested with ketchup that was made with high fructose corn syrup. Ketchups made with other sugars or no sugar may or may not work well.

♫ Extracts

Extracts must be added to the wet ingredients, but add them at the end of the cooking process rather than at the beginning because the delicate flavor of some extracts may be affected by the heat of the hot syrup.

Natural extracts generally taste better, but in some cases artificial extracts are the only option. Use natural extracts when you can, but artificial flavorings are okay too.

Candy

♫ Chocolate Chips

Chocolate chips melt easily so make sure the dry ingredients and the wet ingredients are completely incorporated and have had a chance to cool a little before you add the chips; otherwise, the chips may melt before you get them into the baking pan. Though the recipes call specifically for semi-sweet chocolate chips, you may use milk chocolate chips instead – either one will work. However, where white chocolate chips are used, it is better to use the white chocolate chips and not substitute semi-sweet or milk chocolate chips.

♫ Coated Candies

Like chocolate chips, coated candies melt easily so be sure the dry and wet ingredients are fully incorporated and have had a chance to cool slightly before you add the coated candy. There are many flavors of coated candies available, so you may want to experiment with your favorites. Use mini versions if you can since they distribute through the granola better.

♫ Marshmallows and Other Candies

As with chocolate candies, these candies must be added after the dry and wet ingredients are fully incorporated and have had a chance to cool slightly. Miniature marshmallows are better than regular sized marshmallows that have been chopped because they are not as sticky and are not as hard to mix in.

♫ Sprinkles

Sprinkles should be added after the dry and wet ingredients are fully incorporated and have had a chance to cool slightly. Flat sprinkles shaped like flowers, stars, circles or other shapes should be used, not the small spherical nonpareil type of sprinkles. The round sprinkles are generally too small and get lost in the granola.

♫ Candy Hearts

Candy hearts are very seasonal and may be difficult to find off season. Buy some while they are in season and keep some on hand or look for them on the internet.

♫ Special Note

Great care must be taken to ensure the mixture is sufficiently cooled before adding candy; otherwise, the candy may melt completely, which is not as nice as having the bits and pieces in your granola.

Other Flavorings

♫ Dry Flavorings

Some of the recipes in this book use dry flavorings like cocoa or cinnamon. Dry flavorings may be added with dry ingredients or wet ingredients. Recipes that use dry flavorings are specific about when to add them.

Special Ingredients

♫ Cookies, Pretzels, Crackers

Break cookies, pretzels, and crackers before measuring and adding them to the mix. Put them into a plastic bag and break them into raisin size pieces with your hands or use a can or rolling pin.

♫ Brownies and Snack Cakes

Cut these ingredients into small pieces so they will distribute through out the granola better. The best snack cake to use sounds like "twinkle" and rhymes with "pinky".

♫ Filo Dough

Also spelled "fillo" or "phyllo", this dough is very thin and delicate. Take one sheet and lay it on a cutting board, brush it lightly with melted butter, then lay another sheet on top of the first sheet but **do not** brush it with butter. Lay another sheet and brush with butter, then another without brushing for a total of 4 sheets. Tear the layered filo into pieces and put the pieces in your baking pan. Repeat for a full batch. After the filo is baked, break it up a little bit more with a stuff spatula until the pieces are not much bigger than the other ingredients. Put the broken filo into your mixing bowl and continue with the remaining instructions.

Additional Notes & Tips

♫ Prep

Gather together all of the ingredients needed for a recipe to ensure you have everything you need and enough of each ingredient as well.

Gather all of the measuring cups and spoons as well as the mixing bowl, utensils, saucepan, and baking pan before you begin so you won't have to look for them when you need them. This also ensures you have all of the tools you need.

Keep a towel or paper towel handy. Somehow the stickiest ingredients always seem to be the ones that drip where you don't want them to.

As you use each ingredient, place the remainder of the ingredient to the side or even better, put it away. It will help keep your work space clean and will help you know if you have added an ingredient yet.

♫ Making the Granola

While the dry ingredients are roasting, you can start measuring the cereal and fruit ingredients, then start heating the wet ingredients. This gives the syrup made from the wet ingredients more time to cool before it is incorporated into the rest of the mix.

A small silicone spatula works best when heating the wet ingredients.

A large silicone spatula works best for mixing everything together.

You can use the same baking pan for roasting nuts to bake the granola. Oil it or spray it *after* you have roasted the nuts, not

---

before. Also, even if you are using a non-stick pan you should oil or spray it to help release the granola later.

For most of the granola recipes, don't press hard when you put the granola mix into the pan, just press enough to spread the mixture evenly. This helps keep the granola lighter and crispier. But for granola recipes that use jams, preserves, or other wet ingredients that are not very sticky, you should press the granola into the pan to help the ingredients adhere together better. The best way to determine if the granola should be pressed into the pan or not is to observe the mixture as you spread it into the pan. If it is sticky, do not press it into the pan. If it is loose and not very sticky, press it into the pan.

Allow the granola to cool for 15 minutes or more before turning it out onto a cutting board.

Cool the granola completely before breaking it into pieces.

♫ Clean Up

Soak sticky utensils, bowls, and pans in warm water for a few minutes before washing. They will be much easier to wash.

♫ Storage

Plastic bags or containers that seal well can be used to store the granola. Write the flavor and the date the granola was made on the plastic bag for reference later.

Store the granola in the freezer for long term storage up to 6 months or in the refrigerator for up to 3 months. Some granolas can be stored at room temperature, but any that use carrots, lemon zest, lime zest, jams, jellies, etc. should be refrigerated or frozen.

Index

A

B

C

D

F

G

H

I

Flavoring

K

L

M

N

O

P

R

S

T

V

Made in the USA
Charleston, SC
22 November 2009